# PRIMARY LANGUAGE LEARNING WITH MICROCOMPUTERS

# PRIMARY LANGUAGE LEARNING WITH MICROCOMPUTERS

George R. Keith    Malcolm Glover

CROOM HELM
London • Sydney • Wolfeboro, New Hampshire

Croom Helm Ltd, Provident House, Burrell Row,
Beckenham, Kent, BR3 1AT

Croom Helm Australia Pty Ltd, Suite 4, 6th Floor,
64-76 Kippax Street, Surry Hills, NSW 2010, Australia

British Library Cataloguing in Publication Data

Primary language learning with microcomputers
1. English language — Study and teaching
(Elementary) — Great Britain 2. English
language — Computer-assisted instruction
3. Microcomputers — Great Britain
I. Keith, G.R. II. Glover, M.
420′.7′8 LB1576

ISBN 0-7099-1586-1

Croom Helm, 27 South Main Street,
Wolfeboro, New Hampshire 03894-2069, USA

Library of Congress Cataloging in Publication Data applied for.

Printed and bound in Great Britain by
Biddles Ltd, Guildford and King's Lynn

CONTENTS

LIST OF FIGURES

To Barbara and Christine

ACKNOWLEDGEMENTS

The authors would like to thank:

- Geoff Chadwick, for his good advice.
- Mike Vaughan-Edwards and Barbara Keith for their material on word processing.
- Brian Hodgkiss for the 'Hist Whist' transcript.
- Sandra Pierson and Christine Glover for assisting with the text.
- Ernie Tarn for his material on FACTFILE.
- Dennis Rogers for help preparing children's illustrations for printing.
- The children of Thelwall Junior School, Warrington, for their unflagging enthusiasm.

George Keith and Malcolm Glover
CHESHIRE

Chapter One

# THE FAIRY TALES OF SCIENCE...

An outsider to education could be forgiven for believing that teachers hold two opposing views concerning the role of computers: one, that they are highly desirable and two, that they should be avoided at all costs. Vociferous advocates of either persuasion can be found to extol the virtues of a completely computerised education system or else to deny that the computer has any contribution to make to human development whatsoever.

We may feel that these extremes stem from too much enthusiasm for novelty on the one hand or from the fear of the unknown on the other. Some teachers are undoubtably driven by the desire to take the children head first into the twenty-first century whilst others, perhaps, yearn for a more genteel world which seems to exist only in Edwardian diaries.

The old debate between nostalgia and progress is never far away from discussion about curriculum content and frequently distracts attention from the real achievements being made unobtrusively by those teachers who can quite happily live in the past, the present AND the future. This issue has been discussed extensively elsewhere (1) and having acknowledged it we propose not to be diverted yet again but to concentrate on some of the achievements which teachers from very different philosophies have made in the 1980s.

Bel Mooney, in an article called 'The Grammar of Learning' (2) concluded after a characteristically robust examination of the role of the teacher that:

> ...the art of teaching is identifying what matters in education then working damned hard to interest the pupils in it.

We take the view that, among the things which do matter in education today, learning to use a computer cannot be more important than learning to use the English language effectively but that, nevertheless, there are fascinating links between computers, language and thinking which offer a new lease of life to areas in the primary curriculum that have always been problematical. Traditionally, the primary school teacher is regarded as a living exponent of the integrated curriculum, an ideal which continues to be elusive in the secondary school. With the aid of the computer primary school children can be given opportunities to explore and master the linguistic and intellectual threads which bind the curriculum together.

It would be naive to try to dissociate practice from philosophy but it is already becoming clear that, when teachers learn about and use computers alongside their pupils, practice does lead to new understanding and to a realisation of the old humanistic philosophies which are the ones that matter in the end.

## A LANGUAGE FOR LIFE

The use here of the term 'language' in the singular might well raise a multi-cultural eyebrow especially in the light of the publication of 'The Other Languages of England' by the Linguistic Minorities Project (3).

Human differences and their expression in language varieties are to be celebrated rather than ironed out in a phrase, nevertheless, the idea 'language for life', besides reminding us that education should have relevance to the daily lives of youngsters, also recalls the title of one of the DES's most significant achievements, the Bullock Report, published in 1975.

The contribution of the Bullock Report to a new awareness and understanding of the role of language in our lives cannot be over estimated. What started off as an enquiry into the teaching of reading, concluded as a survey of ways in which language is taught and learned throughout the primary and secondary school curricula. One significant feature of the report was its stress on the inter-dependence of all the language modes - reading, writing, listening and talking. It is interesting to note that the shift from looking at the teaching of reading as a self-contained skill to considering its place in the whole of language experience, has been paralleled by a shift in computer program design from tests of specific skills to open challenges which stimulate language development in more thoughtful ways.

We may have some reservations about the ability or willingness of schools, as institutions, to embody or make effective the spirit of Bullock's recommendations. By 1980 there could be discerned considerable disappointment that the road to implementing Bullock was proving arduous and not always popular despite the continuing esteem in which the Report has been held by educationalists. Often too, it is noticeable that bad practice has a tenacious capacity for survival even when, and perhaps especially when, carried out in the name of enlightenment.

If the Bullock Report recommended a new perspective for teaching literacy it could not of itself bring about the necessary changes in teachers' perceptions and classroom practice. It pointed the way to new approaches to reading and writing while emphasising the fundamental importance of oracy. It also advised on programmes of in-service education. Significantly, however, the Report appeared too early to take into account the revolution in computer technology. It may well prove, however, that the arrival of relatively inexpensive and reasonably plentiful microcomputers has provided just the instrument needed for implementing the very changes in our understanding and our approaches to literacy and oracy advocated by Bullock.

So far the internal revolution in teacher's understanding of language has been slow and sporadic. Reading has undoubtedly received the largest amount of attention in the last ten years. Reading development has been one of the most popular initial and in-service B.Ed options while Open University Post Experience Diplomas and a variety of M.Ed courses at other universities have provided opportunities for an advanced study of linguistic aspects of reading. Indeed the reading research industry in colleges and departments of education had, by 1980, reached proportions equalled only by the output of publishers during the great era of reading schemes. Questions recently set on a Manchester University Finals B.Ed paper reflect an awareness, at least in the minds of some examiners, of considerable changes in the teaching of reading:

- Assess the contribution of psycholinguistics to an understanding of the reading process.
- Discuss the view that the reading scheme has had its day.
- What discernible effects has the advent of microcomputers in education had upon our notions of literacy?

A rather depressing answer to the third question is provided by the observations of an American researcher, Judy Wedman (4), whose survey of computer programs for the teaching of reading published in the United States (1983) shows what is in effect a reversal of the teaching trend in recent years. The bulk of these programs are concerned with phonics and word attack skills while only a tiny proportion are concerned with reading for meaning.

The recent publication by the United Kingdom Reading Association (5), however, of two sets of papers and case studies of the use of microcomputers, presents a much more encouraging view in which notions of literacy are not only expanded but related more closely to insight and imagination rather than to mechanical skills.

Writing, the other side of the literacy coin, is only just beginning to receive the attention it deserves yet it is significant that of the dozen or so projects submitted by LEA's for consideration by SCDC's National Writing Project, 9 to 16, (6) half of them expressed interest in the effects of word processors upon the development of writing abilities.

Oracy continues to be problematical so far as classroom management and assessment are concerned. Numerous studies have demonstrated the value of children's talk but the question of its status remains. Finding purposes, audiences and contexts for varieties of talk in the classroom is not an easy task and the status and value given to interactive talk in particular depends very much upon teaching style, curriculum philosophy and classroom organisation. The Schools Council project 'Investigating Talk in the Primary School' (1981-1983) (7) was shortlived owing to the demise of the Schools Council but a number of its researchers found that, despite the popular conception of primary schools as hives of interactive talk and group activities, teacher-dominated and institutional forms of talk were the rule rather than the exception. They found few opportunities for children to negotiate topics of conversation or to discover their own learning strategies. SCDC's approval for a National Oracy Project (1986) is, however, an encouraging survival of the earlier Schools Council interest.

Primary teachers involved with the use of computers usually report that as a stimulus for talk the computer has proved second to none. Even when the novelty value has worn off it is still observable that some programs generate a high level of interactive talk which, in turn, poses an increasing number of problems for the teacher, e.g.:

- How to deal with the unanswered (unanswerable?) questions?
- How to help children find out for themselves?
- How to structure and divert the individual and group learning generated by the computer?

So far we have identified some areas of language development thrown into relief by the Bullock Report and suggested that change in teachers' perception would need to precede change in practice. We have also indicated where the use of computers might contribute to a better understanding of traditional concerns and responsibilities. Undoubtedly there have been successful innovations in all language areas without any recourse whatsoever to computers and it is undeniably true that any kind of achievement in language development takes time and perseverance both by learners and teachers. It is so often the case, though, that teachers who have made a significant commitment to some aspect of language development (e.g. the teaching of writing or the formulation of a policy for language across the curriculum) are most likely to recognise the intellectual breakthrough offered by new technology.

The internal revolution in our attitudes and approaches to 'A Language for Life' has been modest and gradual in comparison with the external revolution wrought by microcomputers which, in the last five years, has been lavish and overwhelming. If, during the next five years, teachers can bring about a marriage between new perceptions of language and imaginative approaches to computer assisted learning, it may be possible to consolidate some important insights and to implement some very desirable curriculum changes. This may not have been the match we had looked for but the technology may in the end accomplish some old humanistic aims by relating the ways in which we teach literacy and oracy more closely to the ways in which human beings really think and feel about themselves and their lives. After all language itself is just another technology, a human invention, albeit a very early one in man's evolution.(8)

## COMPUTERS

The advice often given to business people when they inquire which computer they should buy is that they should first choose the programs they wish to use and then buy the computer upon which those programs will run. This is also sound advice for teachers. An investigation into the software available for use in education will show that it is run on a handful of favoured machines and that these machines all have a small number of features in common:

- They support colour display when used in conjunction with a colour TV or monitor.
- They are able to produce sound at different levels of sophistication.
- They have the facility to access a fast-loading data-retrieval mechanism such as a disc-drive.
- They can be connected to a printer.

The sound and colour features contribute to the attraction of many educational programs and, whilst not being vital, are especially desirable in programs using any sort of graphic display.

A disc-drive is more than desirable when one considers that programs and data loaded from tape-cassette can take many frustrating minutes as opposed to the seconds taken by a disc-drive. In addition, because of the random accessibility of programs on a disc, it is possible for a program to access a disc and load in information or another program - an impossibility with cassette-based programs. This ability to access the disc at any time adds greatly to the potential sophistication of programs as illustrated by the program suite WORDHOARD, discussed later, in which, for instance, parts of the program are used a number of times and a record is kept of the progress of anyone using WORDHOARD.

There are many advantages in having a printer attached to the computer especially if story-writing programs are being used. Otherwise, without a printer, children would have to copy large sections of script from the monitor screen. Other programs are currently available which will print out text or pictures of work done by children if a printer is attached to the computer. It should also be appreciated that the addition of a printer makes feasible experimentation in the largely unexplored territory of word processing.

## The Computer as a Resource

Teachers have always used resources in their exposition and, almost daily, more and more resources at higher and higher costs clamour for our attention if not for subsequent use. Radio and TV have secured a niche in classroom use but suffer from the disadvantage that the editorial decisions on the content of the programmes transmitted lie outside the teacher's control. This problem can be solved by the use of two further resources - the tape recorder and the video recorder - which enable the teacher, by previewing the material, to use only those parts of programmes which make a significant contribution and to avoid those parts which do not.

The computer can be viewed as an infinitely programmable resource which the teacher can use in any way he wishes depending upon his choice of program and the way he uses it. It would be surprising if, having found TV and radio useful resources, a more flexible tool - the computer - should not lend itself to an even greater variety of applications. What those applications may be will depend upon what the computer program does and what it can be made to do.

Lest we take radio and TV too much for granted it is worth remarking that many teachers have yet to come to terms with the creative use of video and sound recording. Children can derive considerable support in their writing from the opportunity of sorting out their ideas in other media e.g. conducting an opinion poll by tape recorder. Yet children are infrequently found using electronic media in an active way and only too frequently found watching and listening passively. We hope to show how the computer, used imaginatively, can, in fact, give teachers and pupils greater editorial control over the learning which takes place.

Computer programs in education generally fall into one of the following categories:

- Drill and Practice
- Computer Aided Instruction
- Demonstration and Simulation
- Model
- Tool

Drill and Practice Programs. The first educational computer programs to be written were mainly in this category and there must be very few teachers who write programs who have not written either a times-table tester or a spelling tester. As is implied, the program asks the user a question to which he types an answer. If the answer is correct he is congratulated and asked another question. If the answer is incorrect the user may be given a second try and in the event of the correct answer still not coming forth it is printed on the screen.

This is technically the simplest type of program to write, requiring a basic structure in which different questions and answers can be slotted, which probably accounts for programs of this type being far more numerous than any other. It also accounts for publishers, parents and, sadly, some teachers believing that it is the only type of program to have any educational value.

Drill and practice programs do, in reality, have very little to justify their use being based upon the common misconception that education is preoccupied solely with the transferrence of what is commonly thought of as 'the facts' from teacher to learner. Today's teachers are more concerned with concepts and structures, skills and understanding, opinion and interpretation than they are with bald facts. These concerns, however, do not lend themselves easily to testing with drill and practice computer programs and so are all but ignored by many who profess themselves interested in the use of computers in schools, providing useful ammunition for others who wish computers to be kept out of the classroom altogether.

Of course facts are important but often the differences between fact and opinion are presented in a way which is confused or too rigid. Two different opinions, for instance, can be based on the same facts while different facts can be a basis for similar opinions. The same two-way relationship exists between 'persuasion' and 'information'. There is, for example, nothing more persuasive than a careful selection and arrangement of information (or facts!). Explicit argument (or opinion) is often unnecessary when the so-called facts speak for themselves. We shall give an example of children exploring this in a later chapter. It is a pity that the DES document 'English 5-16' (9) perpetuates this simplistic distinction between fact and opinion. One of the things that the computer can demonstrate is the ever-changing composition of facts despite their apparent permanence.

The usefulness of drill and practice programs is limited to testing the results of the learning process and contributes little to the process itself. A times-table tester, for instance, may test a child's recall of a set of mathematical results but is of no help in building up the child's understanding of the concept of number or the operation of multiplication upon which those results are based.

The limiting effect of the misuse of drill and practice routines understandably horrifies the anti-computer lobby. If these programs were the only ones available we should find ourselves very much in agreement. There may well be areas in which a drill and practice routine could make a significant contribution to learning, e.g. spelling and foreign language learning, but teachers have already observed that these areas are often better served by methods other than those of the computer - the spontaneity of human interaction, for example, is often a most valuable component of learning.

Computer Aided Instruction. Programs which instruct are based upon the 'teaching machine' method introduced by the American Forces in the 1950s as a way of teaching certain skills or information to servicemen. A computer program working along these lines would present some information to the user and subsequently tests the user's grasp of the information. If a poor score is obtained the user is given the same information and re-tested.

Instruction programs of this kind resemble drill and practice programs prefaced with an informative text and, as such, suffer the same defects as far as educational value is concerned. These programs may well be successful at supplying information but, as argued above, this falls short of cultivating the understanding and self-reliance which are essential to real learning.

So-called teaching programs lead many people into a view of the future in which children sit in front of their VDU screens soaking up information like so many compliant sponges; and here lies the danger. For in this type of program the relatively unimportant aspects are emphasised and there is the possibility that the curriculum will be subtly converted into those things and only those things which the computer can teach well. What seems now a long age ago, the poet Coleridge sounded a familiar warning. Writing about different types of readers he describes some as 'hour-glasses' who merely pass the time of day; some as 'strainers' who somehow manage to miss the flavour of what they read and retain only the dregs; some as 'sponges' who absorb print very effectively and from whom it can be squeezed out without any noticeable change; some as 'diamonds' (the best readers of all) who are reflective thinkers. If we substitute computer users for readers it is not difficult to recognise the 'hour-glasses' playing arcade games, the 'strainers' and the 'sponges' going through drill and practice routines and computer assisted instruction and the 'diamonds' using the programs which are, sadly, only too few at the present time. Daniel Chandler (10) in this context has remarked that the computer...

> is the ultimate weapon of those who want to get 'back to the Basics', allowing them to process children from 'input' to 'output' in terms of 'behavioural objectives' and 'quality control'. A vast new range of commercial interests is competing to meet the demand. Crude behaviourism in a seductive new guise has dominated the educational software market in North America and (to a lesser extent) Britain since the appearance of the personal computer in 1975.

It is curious that 'basics' are always thought of in terms of 'editing' or 'finishing off' skills, e.g. punctuation, rather than in terms of the fundamental skills necessary for good language performance. The basics, in fact, lie in conceptual thinking rather than in surface appearances.

Many of those involved in using computers in education agree with Chandler and point to altogether different ways of using other types of computer program to involve children in much more 'basic' and enduring learning processes.

Added to this is a belief that children learn best through seeing and doing as stated in the old Chinese saying:

> Tell a child something and he forgets it.
> Show a child something and he remembers it.
> Let a child do something and he knows it.

So rather than being the recipients of second-hand information children should be given the opportunity of first-hand experience. Instead of practising skills for use later in life children should learn skills which are necessary to the meaningful activities they are involved in at the time.

The type of program outlined in the next sections offer opportunities for children to gain new experiences and to use language for the purpose of giving those experiences meaning and significance.

Demonstration and Simulation Programs. This type of program, as the name suggests, uses the computer graphics capability to display a demonstration of some phenomenon which may be difficult or impossible to do otherwise. An example of this might be a program which displays and demonstrates the movement of the planets of the solar system. These programs often have elements of simulation in them which may allow the user, in our solar system example, to introduce some random factor, a comet perhaps, and study its effect.

Demonstration programs, by their nature, are ideally suited to displaying occurrences of a scientific or mathematical nature. One example of this is HALVING published by MEP. In this program, described in the credits as a short film, a square is displayed with half of its area coloured. This coloured area then moves across and around the square whilst remaining a constant half of the square's area. The program thus presents an excellent demonstration of how a fraction remains the same even though its shape changes.

An example of a scientific simulation is one providing a computerised demonstration of Millikan's Experiment which involves showing a charged oil-drop in a rarified atmosphere moving between the plates of a capacitor. In reality, this is a very difficult experiment to set up as it is susceptible to any slight interference. It thus makes an ideal candidate for computer simulation.

Both of the above programs satisfy the aim given earlier i.e. of providing the child with first-hand experience. If the program contains some element of simulation, as the Millikan's Experiment does, the user can try various inputs to see what effects these have on the demonstration thus discovering more about the phenomenon by a process of trial and error.

Programs which simulate experiments are, naturally, not meant to replace the real thing and any teacher of science would expect to set up the actual experiment at least once to prove its agreement with the theory. What the computer demonstration provides is an illustration of the theory and an opportunity for students to explore the potential of the set up with minimal time wasted on irrelevancies.

Adventure games are also examples of simulation programs allowing the user to play a role during which he makes decisions, solves problems and learns by his mistakes within an imaginative scenario. The fact that these programs represent first-hand experience, involving the user in working towards forseeable goals yet operating entirely through language use, makes them of special interest to the English teacher. Chapter Two discusses and gives examples of children using and writing adventure games.

Model Programs. Model programs owe their origins to a method used in the physical sciences which involves solving problems by making and studying parallel but smaller-scale problems - in fact, by making a model of a real situation. A computer program of this type would be composed of many mathematical equations modelling the complex relationships existing between elements of the system. The user supplies data to the program which are entered into the equations and the results given in data form or shown graphically. An example of this might be the model of the British economy contained in the Treasury computer into which economists enter such data as their spending targets. The likely effect on the economy is calculated and subsequently displayed by the program.

Model programs, whilst providing experience and opportunities for activity are more suited to the purposes of the scientists than those of the English teacher. These programs can, however, provide a vital element within the 'class project', that primary school work-horse which, if used properly, can provide a stimulating context for language work. An example of this using the computer model program DIET is discussed in detail in Chapter Four.

The Computer as a Tool. The reasons for the existence of the computer and for its successful introduction into so many fields can all be traced to its efficiency and adaptability as a tool. The early mainframe computers were constructed with very specific purposes in mind, as tools to ease the workload involved in census-taking, for instance. The latest home computers are also marketed with specific, if diverse, purposes in mind; one such purpose being to operate as an opponent in a game.

It follows from this that all programs are simply tool attachments which allow the computer to operate in different ways. If we look at the programs described so far, we find this to be so. Geof Chadwick (11) suggests that educational usage of computers can be seen as a continuum ranging from one extreme, in which the computer plays the dominant role, such as in drill and practice programs, to the other extreme, in which the pupil is in control and uses the computer to do what he requires. The continuum might also be described as ranging from content-bound to content-free programs. An example of the latter would be the creation of a diary or the setting up of a database.

Content-free programs can be used in many different ways within the study of any subject area. An obvious example of this type of program is a word processor which enables the computer to act as a superior typewriter, allowing the operator not only to correct mistakes before printing a document but to manipulate text and design the overall printout without being an expert typist. This book, for example, was compiled using the WORDWISE PLUS word processor program. There are also special types of word processor programs available such as teletext emulators, allowing the construction and manipulation of electronic pages, and newspaper emulators, such as FRONT PAGE, which allow the production of facsimile newspaper pages.

Data-bases are another example of content-free computer-programs in which the user may store information about any subject he chooses and then manipulate and search within that information according to his interests and the facilities offered by the program.

There are also programs which act as support tools and investigation tools. WORDPLAY, for instance, utilises the user's inputted words and produces 'poetic' forms from them; MICROSTORY offers support for creative writing by providing a framework for the story and prompts the user to supply characters, descriptions and dialogue within that framework; TRAY provides an opportunity for language investigation by presenting a total cloze passage.

All tools involve the operator in activity to some purpose and in the process provide first-hand experience. Computerised tools have particular value since they add a new dimension to classroom activities and another source of experience for children and teachers to share. In this way computers can make a positive contribution to classroom work benefitting from an experience-based philosophy which, as we have argued previously, emphasises questioning, hypothesising and testing as opposed to transferring disparate or even packaged facts.

In the particular case of language development a greater understanding of the mechanics of language and a better appreciation of linguistic form results from an approach which enthuses over exploring the possibilities in language rather than one which relies on restricted and restricting language exercises.

## LANGUAGE AND COMPUTERS

By 1983 there could be discerned in Britain a growing body of teachers interested in the potential of the microcomputer for the teaching of what it has now become convenient to call 'the language arts'. The term is a common one in the United States and is becoming increasingly familiar in Britain. It is a useful shorthand for combining what goes on in the primary schools under the heading of language development and in secondary schools under the heading of English. It helps to get across the great 11+ divide by focussing on the common linguistic and literacy concerns of both primary and secondary teachers and, when used with reference to microcomputers, it places the arts and technology in a unified context rather than perpetuating the divisions perceived between them. Primary teachers in general were introduced to the use of microcomputers earlier than secondary English teachers and it is probably true to say that the use of computers was explored first of all in areas of the primary curriculum other than those normally designated 'language development'. The MEP Microprimer pack and Cambridge FACTFILE for example, have proved very influential in this respect.

When, in 1983, the National Association for the Teaching of English (12) held its annual conference at the University of Surrey, and in the following year at Durham, it was plain that a growing number on both sides of the Atlantic were enthusiastic about the use of microcomputers in teaching language arts. Commissions led by Daniel Chandler brought together a wealth and variety of experiment and experience. What opposition there was seemed to be voiced out of anxiety rather than on principle. Stimulated by the debate between computer users and computer shunners, members of the Education Faculty of the University of Connecticut initiated a Delphi Study, to investigate teachers' views on the effects of computer technology upon teaching and learning the language arts. Participants were drawn from the United States, Canada and Great Britain and were asked to complete three questionnaires.

The first questionnaire contained 44 propositions, many of them contradictory, and teachers were asked to predict the likelihood of specific changes taking place by the years 1990, 1995 and 2000. They were also asked to rate, on a five point scale, the desirability of the changes. The aim was to discover in what ways the dramatic technological changes so hotly debated would be likely to manifest themselves and to what extent. Here are some of the propositions directly related to the topics of this book, together with our own comments:

- Electronic information sources (e.g. video texts, databanks) will replace textbooks as the primary mode of classroom instruction. (Without any reference to computers at all the follow-up to the Lunzer and Gardner (12) research into reading has already thrown serious doubt on the value of knowledge and information packaged in the form of 'textbooks'. Note, incidentally, the use of the word 'instruction'.)
- The teaching of handwriting will be replaced by the teaching of typing or keyboard skills. (At the moment children display a wide range of ability in this area. One Widnes teacher working on an MEP research project (13) on the word processor in the classroom reports, 'The quality of their writing, content and structure, has improved out of all recognition. Quantity has increased too. The problem is time - it takes so long for many of the children to type in their work. Yet only the other day I thought I had misheard a boy when he apologised for a piece of writing being late because he had had to write it by hand and IT TOOK SO MUCH LONGER THAN TYPING!'.)

- Reading skills (decoding and interpreting print) will be taught by computers (14).
- The definition of reading will be broadened to include decoding and interpreting all message systems - written, pictorial, graphic, aural, etc.
- Increasing sensitivity to and awareness of the linguistic demands (vocabulary, meaning and sentence structures) of electronic communication will require that language instruction be changed from a study of traditional grammar to a broader consideration of the nature and use of language. (English users of the BBC 'Web of Language' radio programmes will have had some experience of such an approach.)
- As the interrelatedness of language and thought becomes widely recognised, the use of language in argument, evidence, persuasion and problem solving will be emphasised over composition, literature and grammar as subjects in themselves.
- As opportunities for oral language decrease students will become increasingly more inarticulate. (This conjures up a picture of children plugged into machines but see the next proposition.)
- Oral language will be emphasised, especially skills related to problem solving, human-machine communication and interpersonal communication. (This seems welcome provided that the 'problem solving' involves children solving their own problems rather than specially manufactured ones.)
- Slower pupils' interactive language needs will be grossly neglected as decisions are made (and more software becomes available) to increase their drill time. (A worrying possibility and more software for this kind of teaching IS becoming available.)
- Sophisticated spelling, punctuation and style checkers will eliminate the need for instruction in basic mechanics.
- As electronic resources become more sophisticated increasing attention will be paid to complex thinking and learning (e.g. evaluation, inquiry, problem solving, invention, the creative process).
- The word processor will replace paper and pencil as the standard instrument for writing.
- The word processor will emphasise format and appearance at the expense of originality and substance. (But it is, after all, just a tool.)
- Learning activities will increasingly integrate talking, listening, reading, writing and viewing.
- 'English' as a separate subject will disappear from the curriculum.

- Learning will become increasingly independent and tailor made. (But see the next proposition.)
- Learning will become increasingly collaborative as a result of electronic networks and databanks. (Not necessarily incompatible with the previous statement.)
- Acquiring facts will be emphasised at the expense of interpreting and comprehending. (This seems a perennial complaint whatever the innovation.)
- The teacher's role will change from subject matter expert to: manager/supervisor of electronic learning programs; resources manager; clarifier of procedures and values; specialist in small group learning and communication; linguistic trouble-shooter.

All these issues need more discussion than marginal comment and readers will no doubt have already debated some of them. The later stages of the Connecticut study consisted of a fining down of responses and an investigation of questions raised. At the time of this writing the final report has yet to be published but an interim report has appeared which detects, so far as British teachers are concerned, a mood of 'cautious optimism' for the future of computer assisted learning in the language arts. So far nothing more oracular than that can be discerned. Lack of money is an obvious impediment though some teachers expressed strong doubts that significant changes will ever occur in language, learning and teaching. In the last analysis it was considered that the implementation of computer technology was wholly dependent upon the educational philosphy of teachers and institutions. Mechanistically minded teachers will go on teaching even poetry and drama in mechanistic ways while imaginative teachers will always find a way of giving the most mundane material an imaginative perspective.

Given that whatever microcomputer facilities are available their use will be determined largely by the prevailing educational philosophy, we propose in the remainder of this chapter to examine briefly some preconditions which seem essential to an imaginative as well as an effective use of microcomputers in teaching the language arts. We share the 'cautious optimism' of the Connecticut study and refuse to be depressed by the more general awareness of how much language use in classrooms is in any case determined by powerful social constraints and habits of thought.

Undoubtedly the language of teachers IS a dominant influence upon the style of classroom learning and undoubtedly the content of learning is bound to suffer the limitations of the teacher's own 'knowledge packages'. This latter point is not just a question of children being limited to what the teacher knows but one of recognising that even 'new knowledge' can be framed in such a way that children do not get an opportunity to make their own meanings out of it. To compensate for this inevitable bias, emphasis has been placed in the primary school on learning through experience but since it is largely through the means of language that experience is given meaning, the doctrine of experiential learning has in recent years been reinforced by emphasis on interactive learning in which talk plays such an essential part. This in turn has necessitated a teaching approach which makes extensive use of groupwork, resource based learning, communicative contexts for writing, collaboration with parents in reading and more extensive involvement of the wider community in the children's learning processes.

It is in an educational perspective such as this that the language arts and the use of microcomputers can flourish so excitingly.

## A CATALYST FOR LEARNING

In the summer of 1985 a joint working party was set up by NATE, at the invitation of the DES, to examine projects for microcomputers in English teaching and to make recommendations in such key areas as literacy, the teaching of writing, the teaching of literature and the use of computers for language development. The working party consisted of teachers and lecturers with experience and expertise in the use of computers and more specifically in program design, or who were actively engaged in researching developments in the uses of computer technology in the classroom.

During a four-day conference at the Institute of Education, Cambridge University, the working party prepared papers summarising the state of the art in the areas indicated and making specific recommendations to the DES for the implementation of computer technology in the language arts over the next five years. Earlier in the year MEP had held a conference at Roehampton on the influence of computers on styles of learning in schools. Both conferences recognised possibilities for quite significant changes and were concerned that teachers should be able to influence those changes to the best advantage for tomorrow's pupils.

A draft paper produced by the Language Development subgroup at the Cambridge Conference makes a number of proposals for developments in the immediate future. (See Appendix One.) The paper also reflects the concern expressed at both conferences for creative rather than mechanistic learning and discussed computer technology as an agent for social, cultural and educational change rather than as a ruthless force breeding anxiety out of all proportion to its value for human life.

To view the computer as a catalyst for learning is to recognise its capacity for enabling teachers to change the environment of learning in their classrooms and to forge new relationships between the 'world of learning' inside the school and the 'world of learning' outside. With its memory capacity and operational flexibility, the microcomputer draws upon the ability for concentrated attention which many children have usually withheld or never discovered in their schoolwork. Almost literally it enables them 'to see the world in a grain of sand' provided, of course, the microscopic view is guided by imagination. Yet, at the same time, microcomputers have a capacity for generating communication and information networks which offer schools a vast yet accessible view on the macrocosm of human knowledge.

Language, of course, as we shall repeat more than once in this book, has been offering this dual perspective for centuries. It permits very detailed, minute description of single entities yet, at the same time, allows us to carry the whole world around in our heads. Language will always be more important than computers but it is our view that the new intellectual perspectives introduced by computers together with their catalytic power offer teachers considerable justification for calling the primary language curriculum 'a language for life'.

## WAITING FOR DYNABOOK

It's very easy when thinking about the use of computers in education to slip into prophecies of what classrooms will be like in tomorrow's world. Once the name of Alan Kay and the concept Dynabook are introduced into discussion there is a danger that anything teachers may be doing now will seem little more than marking time until the real thing comes along. Nothing could be further from the truth.

Dr. Mike Sharples, Britain's most persuasive advocate of Dynabook, regards it as a significant step towards what he calls the 'intelligent word processor'. He describes it thus (15):

> Let's .... pretend that a Dynabook does exist and it supports a powerful programming language like Smalltalk. It is the size and thickness of an A4 pad, with a detachable keyboard, a photosensitive 'light pen' to draw on the screen and a good quality loudspeaker. It has a plug-in memory pack the size of a credit card which can store the text and pictures of, say, five average-sized books, or five minutes of synthesised speech.

The idea of Dynabook was originated in the 1960s by Alan Kay who, as a member of the Learning Research Group (LRG) at the Xerox Palo Alto Research Centre in California, has worked toward the day when the dream will become an everyday reality in homes and schools. Smalltalk is the name assigned by LRG to the software part of Dynabook. It is a communication system, rather than another computer language, which non-programmers can master and use with relative ease and great flexibility.

In Scientific American (September, 1977) Kay writes:

> The future increase in capacity and decrease in costs of microelectronic devices will not only give rise to compact and powerful hardware but also bring qualitative changes in the way human beings and computers interact. In the 1980s both adults and children will be able to have as a personal possession a computer about the size of a large notebook with the power to handle virtually all their information related needs. Computing and storage capacity will be many times that of curent microcomputers: tens of millions of basic operations per second will manipulate the equivalent of several thousand printed pages of information. (16)

No wonder Dynabook is being heralded as a technological-linguistic breakthrough equivalent to the printing press, the telephone, radio and television.

In Byte (August 1981) Adele Goldberg writes:

> The vision is a hand-held high performance computer with a high resolution display, input and output devices supporting visual and audio communication paths and network connections to shared information resources. LRG's goal is to support an individual's ability to use the Dynabook creatively. This requires an understanding of the interactions among language, knowledge and communication. (17)

One particularly exciting feature of Dynabook is the way in which the screen can display any arrangement of overlapping windows of information so that, for example, the text of a story could be displayed alongside the user's own comments and accompanied by illustration and animation. With the support of a word processor program users will have an extraordinary power and control not only over their own writing but also over any texts and graphics they choose to read.

The vision of Dynabook is tantalisingly close to realisation and promises to revolutionise school learning. When it does appear it is essential that there should also exist a range of good language arts software to go with it. It is our belief that teachers, working with the right kind of programmers, will make the best designers of software. But they will need a rare understanding of those 'interactions among language, knowledge and communication' mentioned by Adele

Goldberg, together with a highly creative approach to learning.

In the meantime, however, there exists a range of software for the BBC Computer which can be used by teachers and young learners with great profit and enlightenment. Waiting for Dynabook need not be a period of hesitancy or inertia but a positive programme of self education. It might be worth drawing a parallel between developments in computing and developments in sound recording. If Fred Gaisberg (18), the pioneer recording engineer and entrepreneur, had had some secret knowledge that one day the digital compact disc would be a reality he might have become very discouraged by the 78 rpm process and have given up altogether. Fortunately, he did not know and the heritage of classic 78s which we now possess, by such artists as Caruso, Chaliapin, Melba, Menuhin, Paderewski, Gigli, Barbirolli, or by the composer Edward Elgar, can never be eclipsed however marvellous the new format may be.

When Dynabook comes it will be all the more welcome to a generation which can look back on the language and learning experiences provided by GRANNY'S GARDEN, WORDHOARD and many other programs ready and waiting for imaginative use.

> Here about the beach I wander'd, nourishing a youth sublime
> With the fairy tales of science and the long result of Time;
>
> When the centuries behind me like a fruitful land reposed;
> When I cling to all the present for the promise that it closed:
>
> When I dipped into the future far as human eye could see...
>
> From Locksley Hall by Alfred Lord Tennyson.

NOTES

1. Daniel Chandler, Exploring English with Microcomputers (CET/NATE, 1983).
2. Bel Mooney, The Grammar of Learning (The Listener, 21.3.85.).
3. The Other Languages of England (Routledge and Kegan Paul, 1985). The Linguistic Minorities Project was a multi-disciplinary research team based at the London Institute of Education. It investigated different linguistic communities in Britain from 1979 to 1983.

4. Judy Wedman, Software: What's in it For Reading? (Journal of Reading, April 1983). Out of 253 programs designed for teaching reading and published in the US (1982), 56% concentrated on word attack and of these 50% was devoted to phonics yet only 5% to context analysis and 4% to sight words. Of the 37% of programs devoted to comprehension 72% of these were devoted to vocabulary building and only 8% to interpretative comprehension.

5. Frank Potter and David Wray, Micro-Explorations (1): Using Language and Readingue Software (United Kingdom Reading Association, 1984).

6. The National Writing Project began in September 1985. It is directed by Pam Czerniwska and the Project Officer is John Richmond. The project is based at SCDC, London.

7. Investigating Children's Talk (Schools Council, 1980).

8. The point is made very well in another context by Jerome Bruner: language is perhaps the ideal example of one such powerful technology, with it power not only for communication but for coding "neatly", for representing matters remote as well as immediate, and for doing all these things according to rules that permit us both to represent "reality" and to transform it by conventional yet appropriate rules. All of this depends on the external resources of a grammar, a lexicon and (likely as not) a supporting cast of speakers constructing the linguistic community. For a fuller treatment of relationships between literacy, culture and technology see Walter J. Ong, Orality and Literacy: The Technologising of the Word (Methuen 1982).

9. English 5-16 (HMSO, 1984).

10. (a) Daniel Chandler and Stephen Marcus, Young Learners and the Microcomputer (Open University Press, 1985). (b) Edited by Daniel Chandler and Stephen Marcus, Computers and Literacy (Open University Press, 1985). (c) Brent Robenson, Microcomputers and the Language Arts (Open University Press, 1985).

11. Edited by Geof Chadwick, David Clements and Philip Crookall, Microelectronics in Your School (Cheshire County Council, 1983).

12. All the papers prepared by sub groups of the working party will be published by NATE and in addition to the topics already mentioned there will be papers and recommendations on information technology and simulations. Timed for publication at the same time as the Surrey Conference was a collection of papers edited by Daniel Chandler, Exploring English with Microcomputers (Council for Educational Technology, 1983).

13. This project is directed jointly by the Cheshire Language Centre and the Department of Communications Technology at North Cheshire College, Warrington WA2 ODB.

It is specifically concerned with ways in which the use of a word processor can be integrated into the everyday teaching environment, with assessing the effects and the development of writing abilities.

14. Lunzer and Gardner, Learning From the Written Word (Oliver and Boyd, 1984).

15. Mike Sharples, Dynabook (1984). A lecture given at the Department of Artificial Intelligence, the University of Edinburgh.

16. Alan C. Kay, Microelectronics and the Personal Computer (Scientific American, September 1977, Volume 237, No.3. p.p.230-244). Strongly recommended reading.

17. Adele Goldberg, Introducing the Smalltalk-80 System (Byte, August 1981, Volume 6, No. 8 pp 14-26). Equally recommended.

18. Jerrold Northrop Moore, A Voice in Time: The Gramophone of Fred Gaisberg (Hamish Hamilton, 1976).

Chapter Two

# ADVENTURE PROGRAMS

The first adventure games were written on early main-frame computers by professional programmers to keep themselves amused during the long watches of the night. Those of a romantic inclination may view these programs as the modern equivalents of the sagas and songs composed in earlier times and which performed a similar function. Many of these original adventure programs still exist, clone-like, in forms written for microcomputers - which either vouches for the quality of the original ideas or tells us something about the standard of later ones.

There is something very satisfying about playing an adventure game; something akin to solving a difficult crossword puzzle or cryptogram. In both, individual clues are solved best by those who can adopt a certain free-wheeling mentality, able to investigate multiple meanings of words and appreciate connections between seemingly disparate occurrences. The adventure game, then, is a challenge.

Many of the best examples of adventure games have few or no illustrations, all communication being written bluntly on the screen, all clues, information and outcomes being contained in often terse messages. Adventure games can be played as a kind of linguistic problem-solving.

The classic adventure game scenario is that of a set of locations, rooms in a castle or planets in space, for example. The player moves about between these locations towards a goal, such as rescuing an imprisoned princess, discovering useful items in the process and dealing with malevolent occurrences as best he can. He does this by giving simple instructions to the computer usually in the form of a 'verb - noun' combination such as 'take lamp' or 'inspect sword'. The significance of all communication being performed in this way will not have escaped the language teacher who will be only too aware of the possibilities of children, having witnessed this form of communication with the computer, can be made aware of the fundamental importance of the 'noun-verb' combination in English.

There are very many adventure games available of the type described above, CASTLE OF RIDDLES and THE HOBBIT being two of the best. Almost any of them could be used in the classroom to stimulate discussion or suggest a scene for creative writing. Such games as these can help to motivate children who are often reluctant, in class, to make a verbal contribution but may do so if immersed in the imagined world of an exciting adventure game. In addition children learn much from the vocabulary and styles of argument adopted by more eloquent members of the group.

The form of the adventure game can also be a source of inspiration to the language teacher. Children, once familiar with the formula these games use, can be encouraged to construct a small number of scenes which they can illustrate. The pictures are then linked together in the form of a simple adventure game using a sentence to set the scene and a question posed to the would-be player, the answer to which decides his fate - transportation to another of the scenes or oblivion. There are available computer programs which are empty of plot in which children can insert their own scenario, characters, scenes and outcomes; the Anita Straker program MAKE ADVENTURE, published by MEP, is one such program. Using this program or a similar one provides children with a new opportunity for creative writing the product of which, a self-written adventure game, can be played by the child or by his friends during which any defects in the writing should emerge and may be rectified accordingly.

As will be appreciated, the experience in language use when children write their own adventure programs can be every bit as intense as more traditional forms of story-telling. There are, however, some additional benefits. For instance, the tasks in writing a game can be usefully dealt with separately. First, a thematic scenario comprising a number of linked scenes must be invented. The second task is to write descriptions of these scenes, necessary but often-neglected operations in children's action-dominated story writing. Next, the characters and objects appearing in the game must not only be described but their responses to specific stimuli decided in advance. Each scene must then be provided with a situation for the player to encounter, a decision for him to make and a set of alternative consequences of those decisions. Since these tasks usefully fall into a hierarchical structure, children's attention can be brought to bear on one stratum of the structure at a time to the exclusion of other considerations. This program is discussed more fully later in the chapter.

Whatever exciting and stimulating benefits arise from writing adventure games the place to start is surely by playing them. A good one to begin with is GRANNY'S GARDEN.

## GRANNY'S GARDEN

GRANNY'S GARDEN is published by 4mation and is available by post.

The program is well suited to the upper-infant and lower-junior age-range, although upper juniors have been known to enjoy the program if they think no-one is watching. GRANNY'S GARDEN can be used by individual children but, because of the way the program stimulates high-quality discussion, it is better used with small groups or even whole classes.

The scenario is that of a magical land, the Kingdom of the Mountains ruled by a King and Queen, which is accessible via Granny's Garden. The quest which the children are set is to rescue the Royal children who have been kidnapped and hidden by a wicked witch. They do this by solving a number of problems within four adventures, the successful completion of each being rewarded with the release of one or more of the royal children.

The program is in four parts which become progressively more difficult. Each part, with the exception of the first, requires its own password before entrance can be effected and each password is earned by successfully solving the problem presented in the previous section.

The program opens with a picture of twelve trees and the children are asked to find the magic one by trial and error. This is the classic hunting on a grid idea used by many computer programs and after repeated use it must be admitted that the novelty can pall. This, however, has been foreseen by the program designer and the process of hunt-and-guess can be circumvented if the program documentation is diligently searched for the key. This is proof positive of the standard advice for operating mechanical apparatus - 'when all else fails, read the instructions.'!

First impressions of the program at this stage are consistently good; the graphics are chunky but attractively colourful and the music varies between an inspired Irish jig and typical achromatic computer 'music'.

The children are introduced to the program's scenario using a question-and-answer format which combines firmness of direction with humour in its approach. For instance, the children are asked at one stage, 'Do you want to go in the cave?'. If the answer 'No.' is given the program immediately returns, 'Yes, you do.'

The main action in this first part takes place in the Woodcutter's cottage, in which we are told Esther is hidden waiting for us to set her free. There are also a number of dangers there to trap the unwary, but with some avid exploration and inspired problem-solving Esther can be found.

Successfully completing this part of the program cannot be done in one attempt since dangers in the cottage are rife and can easily result in the would-be adventurer having to begin again. Most groups of children take five or six attempts before they manage to set Esther free. A conversation which took place between two five-year-olds and a teacher is reproduced in the following transcript. Reading words from the screen was too difficult for the children so this was done for them by their teacher but notice how the children are drawn into the adventure to the point where one of them runs in fright from the room when the witch appears!

Teacher: Now we can go inside but we must be very careful. The witch has set some traps for you. Would you like to take an apple from the tree?

Both: Yes!

Teacher: Keep the apple safe. I will let us in now. Space bar... We are in the hallway. It is very dark but you can see a long stick by the wall. Are you going to take it? Richard?

Helen: No!

Richard: Yes! No, no.

Teacher: It is very dark but you can see a door leading to the kitchen, a door leading to the backroom, a cupboard and some stairs. Where do you wish to go? Helen?

Richard: Stairs!

Helen: Yes and after that we're going in the cupboard.

Teacher: So we're going up the stairs first?

Helen: Yes.

Teacher: Right we'll put stairs in... We are on the stairs, there is a nasty snake here. Its mouth is wide open - I think it wants to eat you. What can you throw at the snake?

Both: Apple, apple.

Teacher: Right, throw the apple... What a good shot, you have killed the snake.

Helen: Yes, killed the snake.

Teacher: At the top of the stairs is a note, it says, 'Esther is in the house, hidden well from you. Look again and you may find, that one broom is now two.' You go back down the stairs... We are in the hallway.

(REPEATS OPTIONS FOR CHILDREN TO CHOOSE WHERE THEY WILL GO NEXT.)

Teacher: Where do you wish to go next?

Both: Cupboard, cupboard.

Helen: We're going to take the broomstick, OK?

Teacher: Cupboard, there we are. We are in the cupboard. It is very cold in here. All you can see is a red broomstick. are you going to take it?

Richard: Yes, yes.

Helen: (EMPHATICALLY) No, No!

Teacher: Take broomstick... Silly, Silly, Oh...
Helen: The witch is going to come! (Runs out of room)
(NOISE OF WITCH COMING).
Richard: Oh...
Helen: (FROM NEXT ROOM) I told you.

A consideration of the skills used by the children in solving this first part of GRANNY'S GARDEN is a most revealing activity. Most obvious, perhaps, are the skills of reading for meaning and learning to communicate. Solving the problems which occur in Granny's Garden has a strong motivating effect upon children and they soon realise that clues to help them are contained in the text of the program - what a comprehension exercise! Some children inevitably 'see' solutions quicker than others and must then convince their fellow adventurers of the soundness of their thinking using as clear expressions of their deductions as possible. Children whose faculties of logical argument are underdeveloped can learn much from the syntactic constructions used by their more adept companions and, using these as examples, can base their own style of argument upon them. The children are also able to construct hypotheses as possible solutions to the problem and are then in a position to test them within the program. Similarly, the children become aware of the sequencing involved in the program's structure and rapidly familiarise themselves with the order in which activities take place and how best to avoid the attentions of the witch.

With the finding of Esther the first part of the game is completed and the user is rewarded with a password which gives entrance to the second location - the Giant's Garden.

The children must successfully cross the Giant's Garden, in spite of the presence of many hazards, in order to rescue Tom. There are, however, various creatures in the garden, namely a spider, a snail, a bee, a butterfly and a worm, ready to help combat and overcome the hazards. Whenever one of these hazards is encountered, the children are asked to choose one of the creatures to help them and, at first, their choice is randomly motivated. Eventually, though, it is appreciated that each creature can be of help in a certain way based upon its individual physical characteristics. For instance, upon being bombarded with nuts, the snail can be of assistance by offering the shelter of his shell while the bee solves the problem of a savage dog by stinging it on its bottom! The children thus find themselves embroiled in a resounding discussion revolving around the characteristics of these creatures, how they are different, how they are similar and exactly what characteristics are required to help with any particular hazard. The conversation of two five-year-olds as they try to solve this part of the adventure is illustrated in the following transcript.

Teacher: Tom is hidden on the other side of the giant's garden. You will need some help to cross the garden. These creatures will help you...
Helen: Oh, a spider.
Teacher: ...Worm, bee, snail, spider, butterfly. You are on the edge of a wide pond.
You will need help to cross the pond, which creature do you want to call?
Helen: Bee!
Teacher: Worm, bee, snail, spider or butterfly.
Helen: Spider!
Richard: Spider, 'cos it'll make a web across it.
Teacher: Spider. (TYPES IN SPIDER)
Helen: If he says no, we'll have to try someone else.
Teacher: Here he is...
Helen: Oh, will you stop spider please, for me?
Teacher: I cannot swim, I can't take you across the pond. I'm very sorry.
Both: Oh...
Teacher: We still need to cross the pond, come on. Which one... worm, bee...
Richard: Butterfly!
Teacher: ...snail...
Richard: 'Cos he can fly! A butterfly can fly over it.
Teacher: Shall we try the butterfly, Helen?
Helen: Yes...But I bet we're too heavy.
Teacher: I will try to carry you over the pond. Hold on tight, here we go...We have done it. Now we are across the pond. Now, we have to go through a small wood...as you set off through the wood a shower of nuts is falling on your head. The nuts hurt, you need help.
Both: Snail, snail!
Teacher: The nuts are hurting you, what creatures can help you?
Both: Snail!
Teacher: Why do we want the snail?
Helen: 'Cos we can go inside it.
Teacher: Inside what?
Richard: (EXASPERATED) Come on, put snail in.
Teacher: What's a snail got?
Both: (SHOUTING) A shell!!
Richard: And we can go in it.
Teacher: Mmm, snail then...There he is. I will be able to help you. Come inside my shell with me. Now we are safe from the falling nuts... Right, we must cross a flower bed - look out! An army of ants is coming, you need help. The ants may bite you. What other creatures can help you?
Richard: The worms.
Teacher: You want the worm?

Helen: No, they'll fall in his hole.
Richard: If the ants follow him they'll get stuck in the hole.
Teacher: Will they? What do you want, Helen?
Helen: I think the spider.
Teacher: Why?
Helen: No, I think the bee 'cos he can sting...I'm just going to get a drink of milk.
Richard: The worm.
Teacher: There he is. It's the worm, coming up out of the ground. You will soon be safe from the ants...

Successfully overcoming the five hazards with the help of the creatures results in the completion of the second part of the game and Tom is set free. A second password is given which gives entrance to the third part of the adventure - the City of Dragons.

In this next part of the adventure game we are invited to attempt to rescue Clare and Anna who are prisoners of the dragons and have been left in the charge of four baby dragons. Four collars are at hand with which the baby dragons can be restrained and the children rescued but the collars can only be put on a dragon if it is first isolated from its brothers. Items of food are also available with which the dragons can be tempted from their cave as is information about each individual dragon's likes and dislikes. The solution is thus arrived at by offering the dragons choices of foods which attract one of their number whilst repelling the others. As with most logic problems the solution is easy to understand once it has been reached. Whilst searching for a method whereby the problem can be solved children's initial attempts involve some trial and error but eventually they find themselves writing down information and organising this into some sort of chart which can be used to crack the problem, thus releasing Clare and Anna and providing the password which allows entrance to the final section of GRANNY'S GARDEN.

The Land of Mystery is the final part of the adventure and, unlike the previous parts, is more akin to the standard adventure game as discussed in the opening pages of this chapter. A map appears on the screen which has five locations connected by paths for the user to explore. At the locations vital information is provided or useful objects can be discovered which may be used at the appropriate time to discover further information or gain entry to hidden locations and, ultimately, the kidnapped children Jessica and Daniel.

Throughout GRANNY'S GARDEN the object is to stimulate language activities - reading, discussion, reasoning and deduction - within a framework of imaginative adventure and humourous invention. The above account, though indicative of the program's possibilities in the primary classroom, does not begin to explore the many follow-up activities which a pro-

Figure 2.1: Esther and Two Brooms by Richard.
GRANNY'S GARDEN.

Figure 2.2: The Snail and the Nuts by Richard.
GRANNY'S GARDEN.

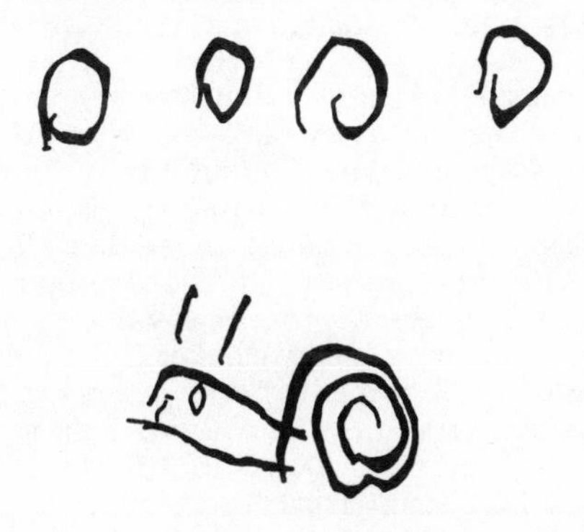

gram of this calibre can engender. The opportunities for art-work alone stimulated by this program could fill a book - witches, giants and dragons are powerful sources of inspiration especially when combined with maps of enchanted lands full of unknown dangers and delights. Figures 2.1 and 2.2 reproduce pictures of Esther in the cupboard with the two brooms and the snail protecting us from the falling nuts with his shell.

There is little doubt for anyone who has used GRANNY'S GARDEN that it not only provides an excellent opportunity for the development of language skills but is also a useful introduction to the genre of adventure games aimed specifically at younger children. It is highly recommended.

As discussed in the last chapter, much of the value of the computer in the primary classroom is its ability to provide experiences for the children to share and enjoy. Certainly GRANNY'S GARDEN provides an excellent experience with its combination of problem-solving and imaginative sprinkling of discussion points laced with friendly humour. This is also true of the next adventure game, SPACEX, which, while it shares many of the characteristics of GRANNY'S GARDEN, extends the range of skills, expertise and imagination necessary in order to reach a solution.

## SPACEX

SPACEX, also published by 4mation, is available by post but is aimed at older children of eight to eleven. The two programs were written by the same author and, as a result, share the same engaging humourous style which children find so attractive. It is surely no accident that the author of these two programs is himself a primary school teacher.

In this game the children play the role of inter-planetary explorers whose starship, the Golden Hind, has left them as a survey team on the planet Persephone. Upon the starship's return a year later the team is horrified to discover that their shuttle, the only means of returning to the Golden Hind, is incapacitated due to the removal of a number of vital components by various members of the semi-intelligent, indigenous race, the Kleptoes! The survey team must track down these components in their land-skimmer and try to recover them from their new owners. In this they are aided by a metal-detection scan from their starship and have the use of a few other pieces of equipment. Figure 2.3 reproduces one group's copy of the metal-detection scan upon which they have drawn their routes. A few preliminary excursions made by the children result in three distinct objectives making themselves apparent.

First, routes must be discovered between the base-camp and the locations pinpointed by the metal-detection scan.

Figure 2.3: Delta Group's Metal Detection Scan.
SPACEX.

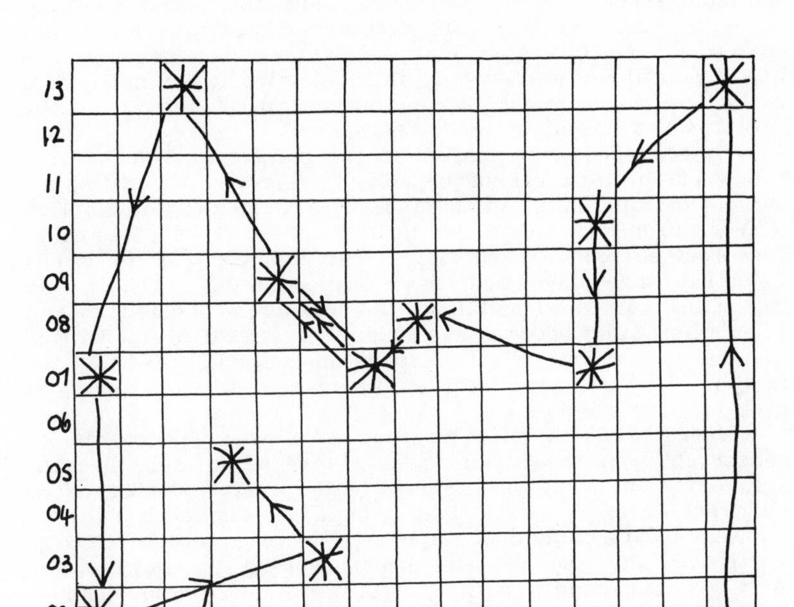


These are not always as obvious as they appear, resulting in careless explorers crashing into mountain ranges, being dragged down by the branches of alien trees or being suddenly bombarded with nuts (seemingly a common occurrence in Mike Matson adventures). In addition, finding routes to some of the farther-flung habitations of Persephone needs long and careful research.

Once into the program the children begin to realise that there is a second objective to fulfil, that of obtaining the required piece of equipment once the skimmer has found its way to a location. Unfortunately for the adventurer these items do not lie readily to hand but must be teased from the situation using guile, imagination and, failing these, previous experiences of the location. Thus strategies must be evolved which enable the users to obtain their goals, failure to do so resulting in the expedition coming to an abrupt end with little choice other than to start again, this time a little wiser.

The third objective is the result of a constraint introduced quite early in the game, namely that the fuel tank of the land-skimmer is a small one. Thus they must find the shortest route between all necessary locations which will enable all the pieces of equipment to be recovered at one time. As will be appreciated, this objective is a final one to be solved as a result of the successful attainment of the previous two objectives described above.

It soon becomes apparent to the players of SPACEX that the whole problem cannot be solved either in one sitting or without making notes of some sort so that information often dearly purchased should not be left to the whim of memory. The most obvious written aid is that of a copy of the metal-detection scan developed as a map showing possible and impossible routes to and from the locations, updated as and when information becomes available. The second useful written material is a record of each expedition containing a list of the locations visited along with an account of what occurred at each location - i.e. a log.

Using SPACEX with a group of eleven-year-old junior school children these two forms of record keeping became, very early on, vital cornerstones in the overall strategy. The children were put into rival groups of explorers and, in addition to the individual maps kept by each group, a large version of the map was also kept, showing the name of the first group to find a path to a hitherto unexplored location. The route to this location did not, however, become public property and this information, together with any information concerning the strategies for obtaining missing items, was jealously guarded and spoken of only in hushed voices.

Individuals within these groups were responsible in turn for writing up the log of each expedition and future journeys were planned carefully and agreed on to enable the maximum amount of information to be extracted. It was after three or four such expeditions that one group of explorers decided that, although the log was an important source of information, the details contained in a number of them was difficult to find in a hurry - such as having to make a decision about the possible hostility of a nearby Kleptoe. This group thus developed a third written aid; that of a list of locations each one annotated with the equipment recoverable, apparatus needed and the strategy to be adopted at each place. This ploy was promptly adopted by all of the other groups of children who saw immediately the power of a crib sheet such as this. The procedure at the end of any expedition thus developed into writing up the log and transferring any new information to both this new written aid and to the map.

Figure 2.4 shows an example of a log written by a member of one of the groups and Figure 2.5 shows an example of the summary sheet constructed by this same

Figure 2.4: A Page From Delta Group's Log.

---

Log 3. Star Date 10th May 2084.

Report logged by Stephen, Delta Group.

Equipment taken: rope, wirecutters, gun, torch, spade.

Visited 0509. Did not stay.

Visited 0313. Did not stay.

Visited 0107. Stayed. The Speed Brake Control was under a yellow tree. A praying mantis type creature attacked us but we tripped it up with our rope and collected our Brake Control.

Visited 0102. Stayed. There was a rope bridge but we did not cross. It was not safe so we used our rope to fix it. We crossed the bridge and found our Altitude Direction Finder. Flying from 0102 to 0406 we crossed a mountain range and a volcano melted our skimmer.

---

Figure 2.5: Summary Sheet Constructed By Delta Group.

---

Planet Persephone - Information

| LOCATION | EQUIPMENT NEEDED | APPARATUS FOUND | NOTES |
|---|---|---|---|
| 0102 | rope | Dirn. Indicator | Don't cross |
| 0107 | rope | Brake Control | Trip it up |
| 0313 | | Manipulator Arm | Stone ten |
| 0405 | | Bean Can | Don't go |
| 0509 | spade | Status Box | South, dig |
| 0603 | | Pressure Gauge | hole no.7 |
| 0808 | | Pressure Gauge | Don't ask |
| 1207 | gun | Pressure Valve | Shoot bird |
| 1210 | torch | Pump | Tunnel 2 |
| 1501 | torch | Boiler Switch | Right x2 |
| 1513 | wire cutters | Computer | Wait |

---

group. Figure 2.6 reproduces a picture drawn by a member of Delta Group to illustrate their log.

After about two weeks of the whole class taking turns, in their groups, to use this program one group came to the conclusion that they had sufficient information to collect all the required pieces of equipment in their skimmer on one tankful of fuel. At their first attempt they failed, made minor adjustments to their plan and at the second attempt were rewarded with a graphics display showing the shuttle taking

Figure 2.6: We Crashed into a Mountain Range.
SPACEX.

off from the surface of Persephone carrying them to the relative safety of their ship, the Golden Hind.

In the overall strategy of solving the problem posed by SPACEX particular emphasis should be placed on the writing of a log and this activity merits further discussion.

There are few teachers of language who would deny the importance of accurate, report writing as one facet of children's writing development. It is, however, difficult to ensure that this notion of accuracy is present in what children actually write. Teachers go to great lengths trying a variety of approaches in their attempts to develop accuracy. Practical approaches necessarily figure highly among them. They might, for instance, take children on a visit thus ensuring a strong base of experience for the children to work from. The children's writing as a result of this activity, however, need not have any adherence to accuracy especially since the children are often, quite rightly, asked to formulate their own thoughts about the visit and base their writing on them. Another approach made by teachers, particularly those of younger children, is that of the children writing a regular diary of their activities. This activity may well pay dividends when used by some teachers but this does not happen frequently in the experience of the authors. Too often diaries contain only bald statements of the activities engaged in by the child who has little or no interest in them now that they are at an end.

One form of experience which often results in good, accurate report writing from children is that of a series of actions such as making bread or mending a puncture in a bicycle tyre. The correct sequencing involved in such an activity is a necessary part of the account and can be tested by someone trying to perform the activity using the child's account as a step-by-step guide. This formulating of information and then using it as a guide to perform similar activities is exactly what is involved in playing an adventure game like SPACEX.

Thus one of the most useful skills encouraged by using SPACEX is the writing of a log which then acts as a repository of information to be used as and when needed. In addition to this the children are using charts and graphs as parts of a larger strategy for the purpose of solving a problem. Compare this, for instance, to children constructing a graph to show how many children in the class have black shoes or brown shoes. The former example has purpose whilst the latter is merely a rather unimaginative exercise in graph-construction. This confirms the findings of many experience-based teachers that children, though learning much from using a tool, learn and understand more if they first construct the tool themselves. In the account of SPACEX the children not only constructed tools - graphs and charts - but realised that it was possible to make a more useful tool - the list of locations, objects and strategies - and then went ahead and made it.

Many of the skills used by the children in their quest to solve SPACEX draw from a number of other disciplines, in particular mathematics, and so the program may claim to cut across the curriculum to some extent. Mention has already been made of the use of graphs and charts in the program but also of note is the fact that all locations are denoted by their co-ordinates in the form of ordered pairs. Children, having once played SPACEX, no longer have trouble in transposing digits when quoting co-ordinates. The program also generates curiosity and interest in astronomy and space travel, the latter now no longer the musings of science-fiction writers but, to the children we teach, truly the stuff of history to be lumped in with Magna Carta, 1066 and all that.

There is also much potential encapsulated in SPACEX for artistic expression: drawings and paintings to show what a Kleptoe looks like or to show the planet Persephone from the orbit of the Golden Hind. As found with the reading of a good book, the absence of illustrations but the presence of contextual clues in the program offers the imagination free rein and allows individuals to create their own, often different, images of the same characters and places.

An unexpected bonus resulting from using this program was that, after about a week of use, the children started to hypothesise. So unexpected was this activity that it was, at first, difficult to recognise. The children, based on the information they had already amassed, began to speculate upon the extent of impassable areas developing on their maps and upon possible alternative strategies for obtaining pieces of equipment where previous attempts had been unsuccessful. Then, most satisfyingly, the children were able to go to the computer and test their hypotheses. There are, sadly, too few opportunities in the classroom for children to experience the satisfaction of seeing their faith in a carefully worked out hypothesis being vindicated.

Playing adventure games such as SPACEX and GRANNY'S GARDEN can give rise to many opportunities for children to involve themselves in language activities and, as we indicated earlier in this chapter, writing adventure games can be similarly rewarding. Whilst it is not necessary to use a computer for playing an adventure game, doing so does remove many of the logistical problems inherent in games normally requiring the use of dice, charts and tables for its decision-making mechanism. There follows an account of a program designed to help children write adventure games for a computer.

## MAKE ADVENTURE

MAKE ADVENTURE is published by MEP and is available from them or through representatives of those LEAs which have licence agreements with MEP.

The program is in three parts. The first part has the same name as the program suite - MAKE ADVENTURE - and allows an adventure game to be constructed to individual specifications. The second part is EDIT ADVENTURE which, as the title indicates, allows any adventure game previously constructed and saved as a disc file to be edited. The final part of the suite is PLAY ADVENTURE which allows any adventure to be loaded from file and played.

Figure 2.7: The Underground Kingdom.
MAKE ADVENTURE.

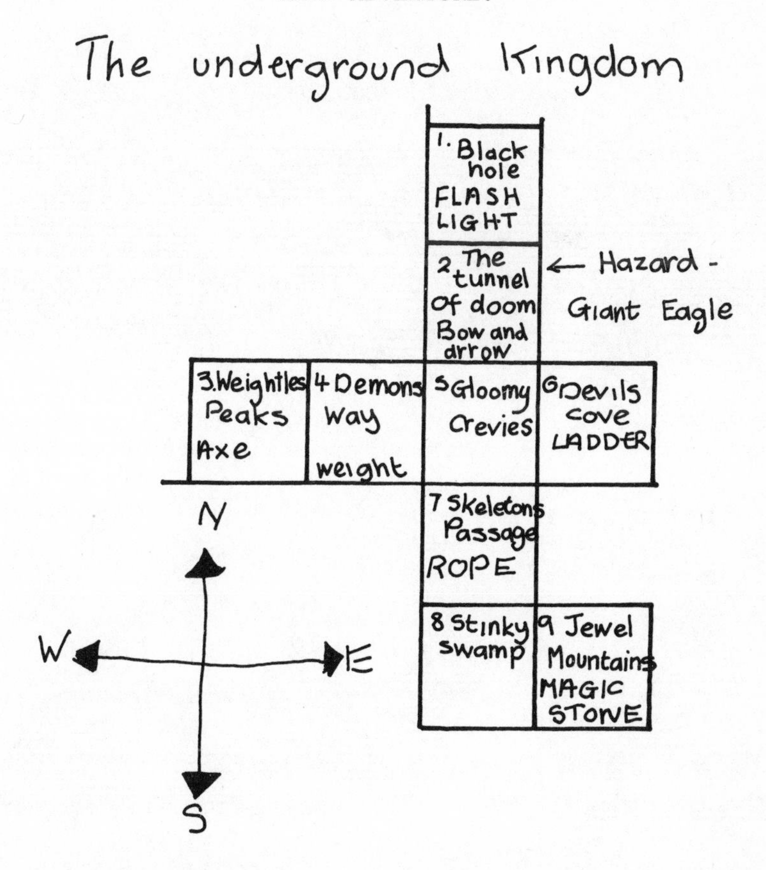

The main part of the program, then, is the first since this presents a creative cutting-edge which can be used by children; the other two parts merely being the utilities necessary to correct mistakes and to play the game. In the following description it should be realised that, in using the program with children, the actual decisions on content are better done previously and away from the computer itself.

The program begins by inviting the user to design a map within which his adventure will take place. This map may contain anything from 6 to 16 rooms or scenes and each room should be accessible from at least one other room - naturally! A group of eleven-year-olds using this program were first asked to decide on a scenario for their game and were given 2 or 3 small squares each and instructed to use them as scenes to construct a group map, each square placed so that it was joined edge-wise to at least one other. Later, when inputting this information into the computer, they are shown

Figure 2.8: The Weightless Peaks.
MAKE ADVENTURE.

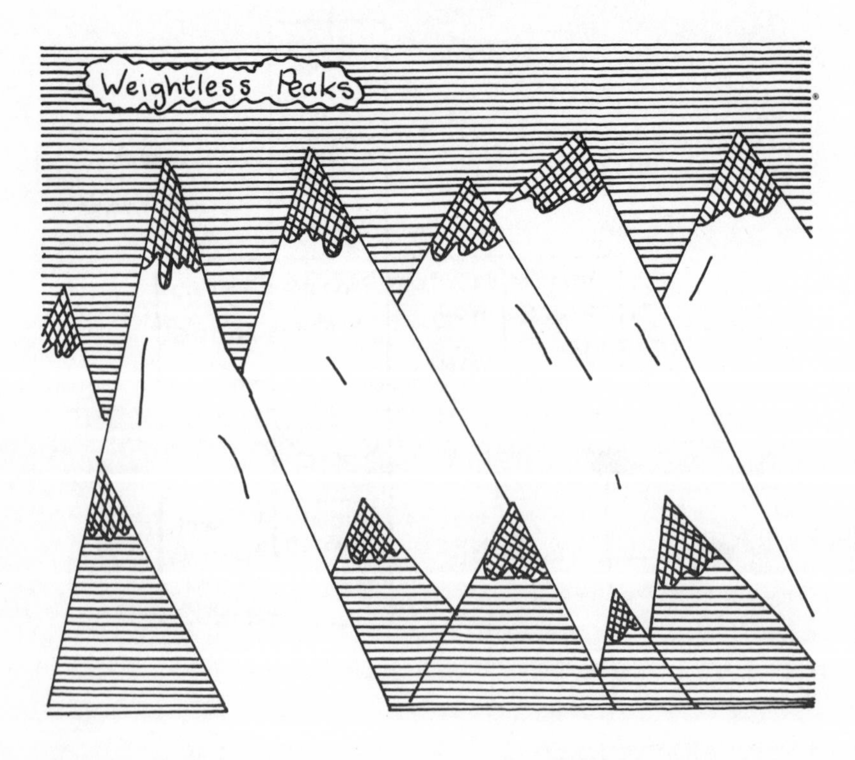

Figure 2.9: Demon's Way.
MAKE ADVENTURE.

a 7 by 7 grid on the screen around which they are asked to move a cursor and thus copy the design of their map. The program then numbers the scenes and the children copy the map and numbers onto squared paper. Once this is done they are asked to decide on which set of direction instructions they wish to use - either up, down, left and right or North, South, East or West. The latter is probably the better choice for older juniors. Figure 2.7 reproduces a map constructed by one group for their adventure game.

The children were also asked to decide on what sort of scene or room each of their squares represented and this description was written on the paper squares. When in front of the computer the children are prompted to type in their description of each scene. Thus, one group of children who titled their adventure 'The Underground Kingdom' had, as some of their scenes: the black hole, Skeleton's Passage and the Weightless Peaks. Figures 2.8 and 2.9 reproduce pictures drawn by members of one group to illustrate scenes from their adventure.

Points are scored in playing the game by finding objects and transporting them to the scene in which the player first finds himself so that the next task confronting the adventure-writer is to decide on suitable objects with which to furnish the scene. The writers of 'The Underground Kingdom', for instance, introduced a magic stone, an axe and a flashlight for the program to scatter randomly about their map. No self-respecting adventure game is complete without a threatening monster or person and in MAKE ADVENTURE the children are asked to invent one who will try to prevent players from achieving success. They will also need to invent an antagonist or talisman - even, perhaps, an antidote to combat its evil intentions.

The benefits gained by children from the writing of an adventure game, as discussed at the beginning of this chapter, are not in any way limited by such a context. Choosing material appropriate to a particular form is one of the skills which lends style to the craft of writing as is that of redrafting work so that the refined product says exactly what the writer wants it to say. Since programs like MAKE ADVENTURE frequently have the facility to edit the contents of a game file, this redrafting element can be an integral part of this type of writing activity. Similarly, since such a program requires the information to be inputted a little at a time, the activity can be similarly undertaken and novice writers given the opportunity to concentrate on a single item at a time to the exclusion of others.

The opportunities for research into specific items arising from adventure game writing should not be overlooked. Children's interest, once engendered, grows exponentially and the information gleaned can add immeasurably to the authenticity and to the style of their writing. Similarly, opportunities for associated art-work implicit in the scenario spring up unbidden and extend further the original experience.

## SOME REFLECTIONS

Dramatic themes and stories have always been an essential source for the language teacher for inspiring children's imaginative writing e.g. setting scenes, sparking off trains of thought, conjuring up a mood. Excerpts from Bram Stoker's 'Dracula' or from 'The Lord of the Rings' are guaranteed, if read with flair, to bring inspiration to attentive listeners. Good adventure games prove equally effective. If there is doubt about this listen to a group of children playing such a game.

Children don't actually play an adventure game; they seem almost to become a part of the game - they experience it. Witness the transcripts of the conversations of the five-year-olds reproduced earlier in the chapter as proof of how seriously children take GRANNY'S GARDEN. Similarly, in using SPACEX, the groups were seen to take the challenge seriously, becoming themselves explorers of the planet.

Experience of children writing adventure games shows the activity to be both cross-curricular yet specific to a variety of individual writing skills. As such it offers teachers of English a valuable purpose, audience and context for creative writing.

Chapter Three

# STORY-WRITING AND POETRY-WRITING PROGRAMS

A survey of programs to help children write stories shows that, in the main, they are concerned with either providing ideas for children to write stories about or suggesting a beginning of a story and asking the children to continue it. Both these ideas are really electronic versions of methods already used in the classroom and in their operation the computer contributes nothing unique to the activity and often less than the teacher would. At best they leave children unsupported, at worst they are little better than Hangman or Battleships.

Teachers whose curiosity had been aroused by the hardware were very early on disappointed by the low educational quality of software of this kind. A few set about designing their own programs two of which, MICROSTORY and POEM-WRITER are discussed in this chapter. Both provide a framework for a story or poem but the children make decisions about characters, plot and dialogue in the one case and about appropriate words in the other. There is also a description of the use of WORDPLAY, a poetry-writing program similar to POEM-WRITER but with the added feature of allowing users to decide upon their own frameworks.

## THEREBY HANGS THE TALE

Continuous writing is not easy. Even the writing of a quite short note can be fraught with niggling doubts about the appropriateness of an adjective, the mood of a verb or the construction of a sentence. Most teachers would admit to having agonised as much over a two line school report as over the construction of their own curriculum vitae. Some times the problem can be resolved by reading aloud, or by talking to somebody else, or even by leaving it alone for a day or two - always supposing that there is time enough.

In conversation, given a reasonably responsive listener, we can retract, revise or amplify what we have said almost instantly. All sorts of signals and feedback from an interlocutor help us to express our thoughts and feelings. Writing, however, is a solitary business supported only by what we can generate from within ourselves or have learned from our reading. Mina Shaughnessy, a distinguished teacher-researcher, went so far as to call writing 'a second language', and so it is, not only to slower learners but to all of us in one way or another.

This chapter is about opening up the writing process and examining it with a finer focus. The micro has provided an excellent opportunity for getting at the thinking that goes on (or doesn't go on) behind a child's written page. It is about encouraging children to think as they write, not we hope in an over prescribed, new fangled 'educational' way but in a generative, enjoyable way which will increase awareness of what can be done with writing by drawing more searchingly on their linguistic resources as well as their everyday experiences. Children's vocabulary and syntax seem best extended not simply by word lists and exercises in isolated routines but by encountering new words and constructions in the context of what they already know or are trying to do. Essentially, any stimulus used should challenge pupils to be that little bit more resourceful or that little bit more responsive to new possibilities.

All of us have mental blocks and verbal short circuits of one kind or another; we need challenges to make us think differently which is of course easy to say and very hard to do. Finding new ways of saying things is not just a literary game but often a way of finding new things to say, of surprising ourselves or, more often in the case of children, of saying things which we never realised other people would be interested in reading. With older pupils, approaching examinations, the problem of verbal short circuits (or habits of mind) takes on a different cast. At that stage in their learning they need to be able to ask themselves, 'Am I saying what I think I am saying?' which can sometimes supply the intellectual jolt necessary to make their writing more explicit or, as the case may be, more imaginative.

Practised writers readily admit, along with the poet Robert Graves, that the waste paper basket is their one essential piece of user-friendly equipment. It receives without complaint, all our mistakes, second thoughts and changes of heart and mind. One thing we can be sure of is that during the process of writing the uncertainty principle is never far away:

- How shall I begin?
- What shall I put next?
- I don't know what I'm supposed to be doing.

Uncertainty stalks any writer whether apprentice or master. T.S. Eliot wrote with great seriousness about the difficulty of writing poetry; he called each attempt, 'a raid on the inarticulate'. The indecisiveness that characterises the mind of one of Eliot's creations reflects the experience of everyday writers too:

> time for you and time for me,
> And time yet for a hundred indecisions
> And for a hundred visions and revisions.(1)

An earlier English poet, Ben Jonson, had some quite specific things to say about the effects of time on writing. His advice to writers in difficulty is:

> If then it succeed not, cast not away the quills yet, nor scratch the wainscot, beat not the poor desk, but bring all to the forge and file again; turn it anew.
> There is no statute law of the kingdom bids you be a poet against your will....if it comes in a year or two, it is well.

Georges Simenon, the creator of Inspector Maigret, when interviewed, had this to say about revision:

INTERVIEWER: What do you cut out, certain kinds of words?
SIMENON: Adjectives, adverbs, and every word which is there just to make an effect. Every time I find such a thing in one of my novels it is to be cut.
INTERVIEWER: Is that the nature of most of your revision?
SIMENON: Almost all of it.
INTERVIEWER: It's not revising the plot pattern?
SIMENON: Oh I never touch anything of that kind. Sometimes I've changed the names while writing: a woman will be Helen in the first chapter and Charlotte in the second, you know; so in revising I straighten this out. And then cut, cut, cut.

Time, or the lack of it, is a problem for both learners and teachers in the classroom. As schoolchildren we were all expected to write to order and as teachers we require today's schoolchildren to do the same thing. Writing is a major educational industry in which the urge to productivity leaves little time for reflection on the process or for revision of the products. The time scale of Ben Jonson's advice, however, despite its wisdom offers little immediate help to teachers.

As a consequence of the pressure of time, of moving ever onward to the next new piece, children are seldom offered opportunity to revise. So frequently do children make fresh starts (in the dubious interest of variety or novelty) that they rarely, if ever, achieve the satisfaction and the accumulated learning benefits which come from a thoughtful conclusion. That sense of an ending, so important to stories, poems and essays is rarely achieved.

Teachers are extremely good at providing stimuli and starting points though it has to be admitted that the beginning is, more often than not, the easiest part. Once the sticking place has been reached yet another great story or great poem fails to get beyond its first line or its opening chapter. We are not using the word "great" facetiously here. Young writers do invest considerable emotional commitment and imaginative energy to their writing and often have high expectations.

The problem with Simenon's otherwise good advice is that children are not usually prolific enough to have anything to cut or shape. This should not however be regarded as unalterably in the nature of things because there are occasions when, given the right circumstances, children will write at great length out of their own personal experience, imagination and linguistic resources.

Some major difficulties then which seem to hinder attempts to get at the thinking going on during the writing process are:

- lack of time
- the need for individual reflection and revision
- lack of a sense of completeness
- insufficient quantity to work on

This is not by any means the happiest of situations but it is worth noting that at the end of the interview quoted, Simenon had this to say:

INTERVIEWER: Is there anything else you can say to beginning writers?

SIMENON: Writing is considered a profession, and I don't think it is a profession. I think that everyone who does not NEED to be a writer, who thinks he can do something else, ought to do something else. Writing is not a profession but a vocation of unhappiness.

Depressing words? Perhaps; but microcomputers have brought a great deal of fun into writing as well as a new opportunity for teachers to provide practical support where and when it is most needed.

When invited to list innovations required for improving children's writing, one group of teachers included the following:

- changes in the environment of writing to create real purposes and to provide real audiences.
- a support system for individuals and small groups which will sustain concentration and involvement.

- some provision of formal structures for writing which will give pupils a sense of the whole and which they can invest with their own meanings or reshape to suit their own ends.

The microcomputer has already gone a long way towards helping with each of these.

We have suggested that programs which provide an idea for children to write about or which supply a beginning to a story are the easiest teacher tasks anyway and such programs will not supply any help to the needs listed above. Nowadays teachers are looking more and more for content-free programs and for writing support systems. This may well precipitate a breakthrough in children learning to write. Teachers interested in some of the problems of designing story programs should read Dr. Mike Sharples' chapter 'A Construction Kit for Language' (2) and also (3).

## MICROSTORY

MICROSTORY, published by ESM and Prestel, is a story-writing support program. It contains story structures one of which, for example, introduces two characters in a setting, allows for a short dialogue between them and then requires an outcome deriving from something in the dialogue. An opportunity is also given for the user to provide a moral to the story and for the end-product to be printed out or saved on disc in such a form that it can be recalled using the WORDWISE word-processing program. The user is guided through each stage of the sequence by prompts appearing on the screen which enable him to make personal contributions at the appropriate time. There is also a facility which enables the basic story structure contained in the program to be changed by the teacher.

When children first run the program they tend to take a long time talking about possibilities though the responses eventually printed in are usually quite brief. With later use this valuable discussion time shows no sign of decreasing but the printed responses become more detailed and considerably longer. The handbook supplied with the disc version gives a number of practical suggestions for extending the use of MICROSTORY and also explains how the teacher may write in alternative structures. Indeed much of the interest, and the fun, for the teacher lies in the prior analysis of different stories in order to discover their shapes.

As much may be learned and enjoyed from the form of a narrative as from its content. Consider for example the delight children get from the repeated patterns of nursery stories such as The Three Billy Goats Gruff, The Three Little Pigs or The Three Bears. Invariably children ask for a bedtime story to be repeated, not just for the sake of staying up a little bit longer, and woe betide the storyteller who tries to skip a few repetitions in the vain hope of finishing sooner.

Children do have a sense of form and an eye for structure. MICROSTORY is supplied initially with a structure known as the fable, an ancient and familiar narrative form which recurs time and time again in modern tales. A 'builder' program allows the teacher to put in other structures but let us consider here an example of the fable structure. In the text you are about to read the words in upper case are words which appear on the screen at appropriate intervals, whilst the words in brackets appear on the screen as prompts. The rest of the text has been supplied by a user of the program.

> OUR STORY BEGAN (WHERE?) under a double decker bus parked at the terminus at the end of our street. IT TOOK PLACE (WHEN?) late one Saturday afternoon in the summer holidays. INTRODUCE A CHARACTER BY NAME Clint (DESCRIPTION) a tatty old moggy (WHERE FROM?) from Corporation Street (WHAT WAS HE/SHE/IT DOING?) was sleeping with one eye open just in case. (ANOTHER CHARACTER) Lotte, a very small cat, from round our way was licking her front paw. CLINT SAID, 'I wish you'd keep still.' LOTTE SAID, 'Stop grumbling.' CLINT REPLIED, 'You're always fidgeting.' SUDDENLY the engine of the double decker bus roared into life and the two cats raced out from underneath. CLINT EXCLAIMED, 'I hate it when that happens.' LOTTE SAID, 'It's a good job we were awake.' (WHAT HAPPENED FINALLY?) The two cats jumped onto the garden wall and watched the bus disappear down the road. AND THE MORAL OF THIS STORY IS: a catnap could cost you one of your lives.
> On completion of a story the program will write a title page such as the one below:

*****************

LET

SLEEPING CATS

LIE

A tale told to
a computer by

Jane, Alison
and Jonathan

*****************

Here is a story written by an eleven-year-old using a MICROSTORY structure slightly different from that of the fable originally supplied with the program. The story is in fact a complete one but the writer was unable to decide on a title and no amount of coaxing persuaded him otherwise. His own title is 'Chapter One' and we have retained that title.

Chapter One

I was stood (sic) in the Market car park waiting for my parents. We had been shopping and we had split up. I wanted to go to the Model Shop for some Airfix colours. My dad said we'll all meet up at the car.
There were lots of cars parked. Our car is an Avenger. Its alright but sometimes it won't start and my dad has to work on it. Sometimes we have to push it which is alright if its facing downhill. I hope it doesn't give any trouble today.
Across from where I was standing there was a Mercedes, W registered and an S registered TR7. I went across to look at them. They were ace. You could see that the Merc went up to 180 miles per hour on the speedometer and it was an automatic. I wouldn't mind having a TR7 though. It was dark red.
The car park had a very low roof. You could jump up and touch it. There was a lot of litter about, cans and newspapers, and a strong smell of petrol fumes that make me feel sick when I am in the car.
I don't like waiting on my own, it gets boring. My dad brought me Warlord so I read that and ate some Minstrels. They said they wouldn't be long and they'd get there before me but they hadn't. There was nobody about. I was the only one in the car park.
Suddenly a lad came up the ramp and saw me. He looked like a fifth former but he didn't go to our school. He was wearing jeans and a jeans jacket. He was tall and thin with short back and sides and he wore Dockys. He came up to me and looked at me. Then he snatched my comic.
'What you doing here? Have you been nicking?' he said.
'I'm waiting for my mum and dad'. I replied.
He got hold of my arm.
'Whats your name?' he said.
His fingers were digging in my muscle and it hurt. I couldn't get free and I thought he was going to nut me.
'You're hurting. Leave me alone.' I said.
He parked me up against the car and I felt really scared. I didn't know what he was going to do.
A car came up the ramp and passed us. As it did I pulled my arm away and ran to the Exit door. The lad ran after me but a man came through the door and he had to let me go. I walked with the man and he couldn't do anything about it.

The man got into his car. What would happen when he drove away. The lad would get me. Suddenly my parents and my sister came through the Exit door and the lad had to go. Was I relieved. My mum said 'Have you been waiting long? You look as if you've seen a ghost.' 'I was nearly mugged.' I told her.
We got in the car and drove down the ramp. It started all right this time.
My heart was still beating and my arm hurt but I was safe. When we drove out of the car park I looked behind and the lad was still looking at me with his fist.

The structure of this story was first 'discovered' by the whole class after a lively reading of the first chapter of Dicken's 'Great Expectations'. When they 'X-rayed' the story, to use the teacher's own word, they found the following shape:

- Pip alone with his thoughts (Why are you there? What are you thinking about?)
- Description of the scene (what can you see? hear? smell?)
- A sudden encounter (Describe her/him/it/them)
- A conversation (frightening? demanding? friendly? puzzling?)
- The parting (and a threat)
- Describing the scene again
- A final thought

The questions and instructions in brackets were supplied by the teacher as prompts for the children's own stories.

There are few details of content in Pip's encounter with the convict Magwitch which can be compared with the car park story but structurally one is an imitation of the other. If the Great Expectations chapter, thoroughly enjoyed as a reading, had been presented simply as a stimulus most written responses would predictably have been about graveyards or convicts. They would have been written in a sterotyped manner a world away from the fresh inspiration of Charles Dickens and equally a world away from the experience (imagined or real) of modern youngsters. The final phrase, 'looking at me with his fist', may have been intended or it may have been a happy accident. Either way it is far too expressive to be altered or interfered with in any way.

## POETRY-WRITING PROGRAMS

Although computers have begun to lose their number crunching image and have become more familiar as writing machines, the idea of using them to write poetry will still seem incongruous to many. Often this is because of an underlying preconception that poetry is somehow divinely inspired and not really the language or ordinary mortals. In this view poetry is more akin to religion and what could be more alien to traditional religious beliefs than the modern invention of the microcomputer! Yet, ironically, language itself is a human invention albeit an ancient one, while the writing system is a technological development of language. Some contemporary poets do of course use word processors and computer programs. Edwin Morgan, for example, became well known for his typographical experiments which are at once abstract and concrete poetry.

One important aim for using poetry-writing programs is to help children think imaginatively and use language creatively. At the same time children will begin to develop a more explicit understanding of the grammar which they already know and use intuitively. Difficulties can arise however if poetry is introduced cold and out of context. Children may not know, for example, what they are supposed to be doing, or they may simply carry out a series of instructions automatically without any commitment. It was because of these problems that we devised an introductory strategy, namely exploring the idea of an 'empty poem'.

## The 'Empty Poem'

Lying behind the use of MICROSTORY is an understanding of narratives as mythic shapes or thought patterns in which we construct and re-tell our experiences. Supposed differences between fact and fiction are irrelevant to the reality, the truth or the power invested by children in their stories.

Ancient story patterns recur in the most modern of everyday conversations and gossip. Everybody has a story to tell. Children intuitively act out these shapes in their improvised drama and do not seem to have much difficulty grasping the idea of 'X-raying' a story. They also enjoy changing the shape of a MICROSTORY just to see what happens. Another notion which children will respond to equally well is that of 'the empty poem' which, in some respects, is an extension of word deletion activities.

The use of word deletion as an activity to stimulate thoughtful reading is by now a familiar one. Originally, under the name of cloze procedure, the technique was used as a reading test in which a numerically determined sequence of words was deleted from the text, e.g. every fifth or seventh word, regardless of its grammatical function. The technique has now been extended as a learning activity rather than a reading test and deletions are made according to linguistic or stylistic criteria appropriate to the particular text. One program designed by Bob Moy for ILEA called DEVELOPING TRAY presents on the screen a total cloze passage, displaying no words at all merely the passage's punctuation. This program is discussed further in chapter six.

Presenting the structure of a poem in which practically all nouns, adjectives, verbs and adverbs have been removed offers some interesting possibilities. Consider, for example, the following five-line 'empty poem':

The ***** ***** ***** *****.
It ***** like a ***** *****.
***** the ***** ***** *****,
A ***** ***** in the *****.
And all is ***** and *****.

In this 'poem' each set of asterisks represents any word which could be inserted so that the piece would make sense. Certain restrictions apply, however, in that neither prepositions nor conjugations of the verbs 'to be' or 'to have' may be used. The pattern behind this structure is as follows:

The adjective noun verb adverb.
It verb like a (an) adjective noun.
Adverb the adjective noun verb,
A adjective noun in the noun.
And all is noun and noun.

Without knowledge of this pattern and given the restrictions stated above attempts to find possible solutions make considerable demands.

At first sight the structure appears to be so open that almost any collection of words of the appropriate word class would give us a solution to the problem. In practice, the boundary conditions created by the syntactic structures of the English language together with the need for cohesion make it necessary for children to think very carefully about their choice of words. Consider, for example, the following possible first line suggested by a group of children:

The silly clown strikes again,

Reference to the original pattern shows that this suggestion appears to be a perfectly good solution to the first line of our poem. However, a glance at the second line shows that it cannot be since the second line begins with the word it and refers to the subject of the sentence contained in the first line. Thus the first solutions have created a disagreement in the space of two lines. Trial and error reveals that the first line of the poem must not contain a person as its subject; this is the first boundary condition.

Children often discover this by the deceptively simple method of reading the lines out loud and becoming dissatisfied with the way they sound. It is many teacher's experience that children also discover their own grammatical mistakes by reading their writing aloud rather than by 'revising' silently. In consequence of such experiments the first line has to be removed and new suggestions made. Below is printed the first complete solution which satisfied one of the children.

The famous circus comes again.
It looks like a Chinese hat.
Quickly the fierce lions run.
A happy day in the circus,
And all is merry and bright.

Notice that the last line is rather generalised. Reference to the original 'empty poem' strucure reveals that the children have chosen to regard as adjectives two of the missing words originally planned as nouns. The latter alternative seems to give a stronger expressiveness to the verse. When this was pointed out to the children they produced the following suggestion which has a far more concrete and vivid last line than the first suggestion:

The famous circus comes again.
It looks like a Chinese hat.
Quickly the fierce lions run.
A happy day in the circus,
And all is sawdust and smells.

By using this approach children become involved in detailed discussions about the meaning of words. Each word is critically appraised, accepted or rejected accordingly.

The model we have constructed is a useful one to use for examining the purpose each word is serving in the poem and for introducing its correct grammatical name. Some of the words, for instance, are being used to name things and can be described as nouns whilst the words which qualify things may be introduced as adjectives; and so on. Experienced teachers will already be aware of how much linguistic ingenuity is needed on their part to make grammatical terminology comprehensible to young children. Instead of working from the labels to the words in context the approach advocated here works in the opposite direction i.e. it looks at the jobs words are doing and tries to categorise those jobs.

Completing the empty poem is a short step from wondering if any noun can be used in any noun space to trying this out experimentally. Suppose, for example, in an empty poem a child needed a verb and could choose one at random from a list together with a random adverb. He would probably find some surprising juxtapositions. Sometimes the effect would be nonsensical, sometimes surrealistic and sometimes intriguing enough to be the germ of an original and expressive idea.

The notion of random choices forms the basis of the program we shall discuss next - POEM-WRITER.

POEM-WRITER

The program, when run, asks the user to provide ten nouns, five adjectives, five verbs and five adverbs and then produces any number of randomly-generated poems, using these words, to the same pattern as the 'empty poem' discussed above. Much depends upon the liveliness and range of the children's preliminary explorations otherwise there is a danger of achieving little more than 'gigo' i.e. garbage in, garbage out, to use the dialect of computer enthusiasts. A fair amount of 'garbage' will probably be in evidence anyway but, since the computer can produce 'poems' in a fraction of a second, they can be just as effortlessly ignored.

Within the program it is also possible to save the words which have been entered as a file on disc and called up by the program at a future date.

POEM-WRITER and Two Green Bottles. A program like POEM-WRITER should be viewed as a tool and, since it is nonsense to use any tool in a vacuum - that is just for the sole purpose of using it - we must use the program within a wider context such as a project or an investigation. The particular context used in this case was the investigation of two green bottles.

The children were introduced to two bottles originating from the 1920's or 1930's of the type commonly found on old rubbish tips where land is being re-developed. They were of light-green bottle glass with various inscriptions concerning the makers and the efficacy of their previous contents! One bottle was slightly more modern in appearance, having a screw-top, whilst the other had a 'popolly'-type neck encapsulating a glass ball stopper - the 'popolly'. See Figure 3.1 for one child's illustration of one of these bottles.

The bottles were passed around among the children, examined visually, touched and weighed in the hand. Discussion ensued about the purpose of the bottles, what the writing on them meant, why one of them was inscribed with an anchor, and how the popolly stopper worked. The children were encouraged to describe their impressions of how the bottles felt and how they looked.

After the children had examined the bottles and commented on them they were asked to contribute words from their own descriptions which could be collected into general lists; first a list of nouns, then one of adjectives, one of verbs and one of adverbs. After much discussion the list reproduced in Figure 3.2 was compiled.

Figure 3.1: The Green Bottle by Debbie.
POEM-WRITER.

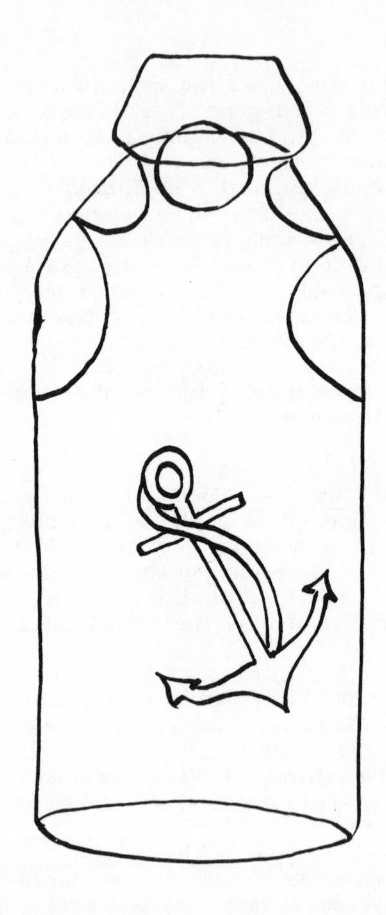

The POEM-WRITER program was run and the list below carefully typed into the computer which promptly responded by producing, at an alarming rate, random poems on the subject of glass bottles. As expected, the offerings varied in quality but, even in poor specimens, a chance positioning of words often produced an unusual, oblique and interesting perspective.

An example of the sort of random poem produced by POEM-WRITER is reproduced in Figure 3.3.

Figure 3.2: A Class List of Words for Bottles Topic.

| NOUNS | ADJECTIVES | VERBS | ADVERBS |
|---|---|---|---|
| rim | noisy | sips | quietly |
| bottle | glass | drinks | carefully |
| neck | heavy | pours | quickly |
| anchor | transparent | shakes | clearly |
| stopper | green | holds | slowly |
| popolly | | | |
| base | | | |
| glass | | | |
| writing | | | |
| bubble | | | |

Figure 3.3: An Example of the Green Bottle Composition Generated by POEM WRITER.

```
The noisy bottle shakes quietly.
It holds like a green anchor.
Slowly the glass neck pours,
A glass rim in the popolly,
And all is rim and base.
```

The children greeted each new composition with profound and, at first, uncritical gusto. However, using the test of reading aloud, 'silly ones' were discovered and reluctantly discarded as were any words which figured too often. Before long the children became enthusiastic critics, each fresh computer-composition having its advocates and detractors ready to put their respective arguments concerning the meanings of the words and phrases appearing on the screen.

The often doubtful outpourings of the computer had become a focus for heated debate about words - their meanings and the nuances implied in odd juxtapositions of pairs of quite common words.

As will be appreciated the children had been involved in a demanding and detailed project of work, including a discussion and evaluation of individual words and phrases, all stemming from a fairly unsophisticated poetic pattern. It would be reasonable to suppose that, given a program which produced more complex patterns, an even wider and richer experience would result and it was with this supposition in mind that the children were introduced to WORDPLAY.

## WORDPLAY

The Program WORDPLAY is published by MEP in one of their Primary Language Packages and is available in the Public Domain to local authorities subscribing to MEP or to its successor (1986).

The idea of the program can seem reassuringly simple, stunningly incomprehensible or mechanistic heresy, depending upon your point of view about poetry. WORDPLAY 'writes' poems from words typed into it by the user in a similar manner to POEM-WRITER.

The program does not and cannot provide any creative input to a poem but, instead, merely makes a random choice of elements contributed by users. It does this by requiring them to input a number of nouns, adjectives, verbs and adverbs which then comprise four banks of words available to the computer under headings. The operator also specifies a pattern to which he would like the poems written by typing 'adjective noun verb adverb', for instance or 'noun verb, noun verb' or, indeed, any number of permutations of word classes. Thus, in the first example, an adjective is chosen from the adjective bank; a noun is chosen from the noun bank and so on until words to fit the whole pattern have been chosen and the complete pattern printed on the screen.

The computer is functioning here as an automatic poem generating machine though whether the results can be dignified with the title poetry is a matter for discussion especially when it is considered that no lexical choices or editorial decisions have been made by the user. Random arrangements of words can nevertheless stimulate ideas whereby the process of rearranging, deleting and making alternative choices, especially in small groups, generates extremely thoughtful uses of language.

It will be appreciated that using this particular program in an incidental, decontextualised way ('today we're going to use WORDPLAY') will not be very satisfactory. Its use is best incorporated into an investigation or project in which children will have prior knowledge and experience to draw upon and which has already expanded their vocabulary. Another essential precondition is that the children should have some notion of word classes i.e. what constitutes a verb, adverb, adjective, noun. These notions will undeniably strengthen in children's minds once they have used the program.

WORDPLAY and Minibeasts. This account of the use of WORDPLAY is based on the experience shared with 28 nine-year-olds.

The children had already worked with the 'empty poem' idea discussed earlier and had also used POEM-WRITER, a program not unlike WORDPLAY but which only produces one pattern of poem. They had also just completed a project on

'Minibeasts', a topic which involved the study of any small non-mammals by means of 'Minibeast Hunts' i.e. going outdoors and catching anything which moves and returning to the classroom to identify, classify, study and sketch what they had found. The children's accumulated first-hand knowledge of their subject provided an ideal opportunity for further exploration using WORDPLAY.

The class was divided into groups of four children, each group having a scribe who was given a sheet of paper divided into four columns and headed 'noun', 'adjective', 'verb' and 'adverb'. Each child in the group made a copy of this and after a reminder and discussion of the meaning of the words was asked to think of four examples in each column based on experiences with Minibeasts. When this was completed each member of the group in turn volunteered a word from his/her list which was then scrutinised by the rest of the group to ascertain its suitability for the group's main list and whether it had been placed in the correct column or not! In a similar manner, by class discussion a list containing the most suitable words was drawn up. This list is reproduced in Figure 3.4.

Figure 3.4: A Class List of Words for Minibeasts Topic.

| NOUNS | ADJECTIVES | VERBS | ADVERBS |
|---|---|---|---|
| weevil | shiny | crawls | slowly |
| eggsack | yellow | jumps | quickly |
| earwig | jointed | walks | carefully |
| eye | spiky | climbs | swiftly |
| thorax | skinny | wobbles | cunningly |
| tail | hairy | dies | dramatically |
| abdomen | small | runs | heavily |
| ladybird-larva | black | flies | silently |
| segment | spotted | slithers | sausage-like |
| leg | sticky | scuttles | steadily |
| pupa | glistening | shakes | cautiously |
| head | | looks | |
| metamorphosis | | flutters | |
| wing | | hovers | |

During the discussion leading to the compilation of Figure 3.4 a number of linguistic points arose which prompted animated arguments between the children before they were resolved.

For example, included in the original Figure 3.4 were various mismatches of tense and person in the lists of nouns and verbs. This was discovered by children while pretending to be themselves a computer constructing sentences in the form adjective-noun-verb-adverb and using words from the lists. They found that 'they don't sound right together, do they?' and after much trial and error it decided to make all nouns singular and to put the verbs in the present tense. This decision was taken only after all configurations of words had been tried and tested. Frequently heard were expressions along the lines of 'Well, we want it to write poems which sound right, don't we?'. There was no doubt that the responsibility of 'helping' the computer to achieve something proved to be a significant motivating factor during this activity. The children were, in fact, the experts and not the computer.

Eventually, when these initial problems had been overcome, the lists contained in Figure 3.4 were typed into the computer and saved on disc for further use. The program was then run and various random poems produced. Some examples of these compositions are given in Figure 3.5.

Figure 3.5: Examples of Minibeast Compositions Generated by WORDPLAY

---

```
Abdomen scuttles, earwig flies,
Sticky black thorax climbs,
Pupa dies slowly.

Segment flies,
Segment scuttles, thorax scuttles,
Jointed pupa flutters steadily.
Weevil shakes
Abdomen flutters cunningly.
Yellow jointed leg climbs.

Abdomen slithers,
Egg-sack flutters heavily,
Leg flies slowly,
Hairy ladybird larva carefully runs.

Yellow spiky weevil slithers,
Glistening shiny abdomen jumps,
Spiky tail looks steadily.
```

---

Inevitably, when dealing with randomly-generated sequences of words, some of what is produced can only be regarded as grammatically-correct nonsense - even allowing for a certain surrealism! 'Spiky tail looks steadily' and 'Leg flies slowly' being obvious examples. However, these occurrences are easily eradicated from the available examples and those which are left do, at least, consist of phrases and sentences which make sense.

A further editorial operation is to collect together sequences which have words or ideas in common. Here we are totally at the mercy of chance but, as remarked earlier, this can be turned to advantage as randomly-derived sequences often turn up combinations of ideas previously not considered.

Both of these editorial procedures are usefully performed by writing each line on a strip of paper and rearranging and discarding until the editor is satisfied with the results. This operation could just as easily be performed on a word-processor but, at the time, one was not available.

An example of a poem produced in this way is given in Figure 3.6.

Figure 3.6: A Poem Composed from Lines Chosen from Figure 3.5.

```
Abdomen scuttles, earwig flies,
Yellow spiky weevil slithers.

Segment scuttles, thorax scuttles,
Sticky black thorax climbs.

Abdomen slithers,
Abdomen flutters cunningly.

Pupa
      dies

            slowly...
```

<u>Further Work with WORDPLAY</u>. Having seen their individual work combined into a class composition the children were now eager to work in smaller groups on topics which interested them personally. They set to work, in groups of four, studying subjects such as railway engines, flowers and animals. Lists of words were produced as before, discussed widely and entered into the computer. A pageful of the program's outpourings was copied down by each member of the group and, working in pairs, they produced two different compositions by rearranging strips of paper and by making further lexical changes wherever they thought necessary.

The program had thus changed its role from being an interesting experiment in playing with language to that of a resource capable of being used in a variety of situations and circumstances.

Figures 3.7, 3.8 and 3.9 are reproduced representing the stages of work gone through by one group of children. These show clearly the transition from lists of words on the subject of dogs through the random compositions produced by the program to the final version favoured by the group.

Figure 3.7: A Group List of Words for Dogs Topic.

| NOUNS | ADJECTIVES | VERBS | ADVERBS |
|---|---|---|---|
| basset | lazy | pounds | swiftly |
| setter | red | jumps | bouncily |
| whippet | skinny | races | lightly |
| spaniel | patches | walks | silently |
| retriever | hairy | sniffs | softly |
| leg | short | hears | nicely |
| nose | long | scratches | sharply |
| ear | black | pounces | high |
| claws | hole | sees | cautiously |
| foot | white | stands | slowly |
| face | long-haired | sprints | quickly |
| paws | smooth | dives | noisily |
| pads | soft | sits | far |
| teeth | brown | stays | handsomely |
| collie | shiny | begs | proudly |
| eyes | rough | springs | |
| | | plods | |

Figure 3.8: Examples of Compositions Generated by WORDPLAY from Figure 3.7.

Hairy brown collie sprints,
Whippet dives,
Setter sniffs high,
Red face jumps silently,
Shiny tooth,
Short paw,

Foot hears, claw springs,
Tooth jumps, whippet sprints,
Soft white leg begs,
Skinny setter,
Brown ear scratches silently,
Rough basset walks proudly.

Figure 3.9: A Poem Composed from Lines Chosen from Figure 3.7.

---

DOGS

Hairy brown collie sprints,
Shiny tooth,
Short paw,
Soft white leg begs,
Whippet dives,
Tooth jumps, whippet sprints,
Brown ear scratches silently.
Setter sniffs high,
Rough basset walks proudly.
Rachel and Debbie

---

## SOME REFLECTIONS

MICROSTORY provides children with a framework within which their attention is concentrated on important decisions concerning the progress of their story. Used in a slightly different way the program can provide a platform for exploring the 'shapes' of short stories which the children can use as models in their own writing.

POEM-WRITER and WORDPLAY both engineer situations in which children's attention can be focussed on the use of words. In addition the programs allow children to make editorial decisions about compositions constructed by the computer but which use the children's own words.

All of these programs stimulate extremely lively and committed discussion about the meanings of words and about their grammatical functions. The programs loosen up the mind, as it were, encouraging it to play with words and ideas. They widen verbal horizons and provoke experimentation whilst, at the same time, reinforcing the importance of considered choices and thoughtful compositions.

We do not suggest that all story-writing and poetry-writing should be done in this way or, indeed, in any way using computers. To be so single-minded would be to impoverish language teaching by removing too many imaginative, exciting or spiritual approaches adopted by teachers wishing to share an awareness and love of language with their pupils.

## REFERENCES

1. Eliot, T.S. Prufrock - 1917 (Faber, 1974).
2. Sharples, M. (1983) 'A Construction Kit for Language' in Exploring English with Microcomputers (MEP).
3. Sharples, M. (1985) Cognition, Computers and Creative Writing (Ellis Horewood).

Chapter Four

# PROJECT-BASED PROGRAMS

Project-based methods are used in many primary classrooms as an alternative to the more traditional subject-based methods. Primary teachers point to the constraints experienced by their colleagues in secondary schools who, because of the necessities of rigid timetables and examination syllabuses, need to work strictly within the bounds of their teaching subjects. Frequently, the exploration of some item of interest crosses the boundaries of various subjects and it seems short-sighted to stop on the promising threshold of a new topic without very good reason. Primary teachers are in a more flexible position than secondary counterparts and are at liberty to follow through that topic without having to pay attention to the boundaries which mark one subject off from another.

The spheres of interest of primary school projects are many and varied. They may be wholly within the boundaries of a particular subject, as many history and science projects are, or they may draw from a number of different subjects across the curriculum. An example of the inter-disciplinary approach would be a study of the area in which the children live and which would require them to develop expertise within the domains of english, history, geography, mathematics and science.

Much of what is done in the primary school is directed toward the development of children's skills in the use of language whilst, at the same time, fostering an enjoyment of language and literature.

Project work presents an unparalleled opportunity for two aspects of language development: one, it demands a variety of language uses (reading, writing, listening and talking) and two, it teaches about different forms in which language and knowledge may be communicated. As a way of learning the project method reflects many aspects of everyday life in which we frequently have insights and make connections without actually being tutored. The chief problem with project work lies in the teaching which makes heavy demands on the resourcefulness, imaginativeness, knowledge and sheer stamina of the individual teacher.

Critics are fond of pointing out how most children, left to their own devices, merely copy out vast chunks of text from any book on hand which may have only the slightest connection with the topic. Undoubtably many children do sift aimlessly through reference books, making copious notes and, unwittingly, do base their writing on an unconsidered selection of information, frequently omitting things which are centrally important. Done in this way a project can become the trivial pursuit par excellence!

Many teachers will already know Jan Mark's 'Thunder and Lightnings' in which Victor, an already 'experienced' project writer, initiates Andrew, the new boy, into a new brand of confidence trickery.

> 'Miss Beale said you would show me round, to look at the projects,' said Andrew.
>
> 'Why, do you want to copy one?', asked Victor, lifting a strand of hair and exposing one eye. 'You could copy mine, only someone might recognise it. I've done that three times already.'
>
> 'Whatever for?' said Andrew. 'Don't you get tired of it?'
>
> Victor shook his head and his hair...
>
> ...'I do fish, every time. Fish are easy. They're all the same shape.'
>
> 'No, they're not,' said Andrew.
>
> 'They are when I do them,' said Victor. He spun his book round, with one finger, to show Andrew the drawings. His fish were not only all the same shape, they were all the same shape as slugs. Underneath each drawing was a printed heading: BRAEM; TENSH; CARP; STIKLBAK; SHARK. It was the only way of telling them apart. The shark and the bream were identical, except that the shark had a row of teeth like tank traps.

The above conversation may be fictional but sadly its factual counterpart is only too evident in primary schools.

The situation illustrated here by Jan Mark is indicative of the shortcomings of the teacher rather than of the project method. Children who diligently copy sections from books or who snap up trifles magpie-like, either do not understand what they are doing or are not receiving enough support from their teacher. In the end, it is the support and guidance given by the teacher, rather that the explicit teaching method adopted, which will determine the quality of work produced by the children. In project-based work, where the children are operating alone for much of the time, it is especially important that they should be given guidance along the following lines:

- There should be an overall aim to the project of which the child is aware and to which he can work toward.
- Children's contributions to a project should be sequenced in such a way that they know what they are doing at each stage and can judge the relevance of information at any particular stage.
- Children should have ample opportunity to discuss work in progress among themselves, and with the teacher, before writing it, and should have clear purposes and audiences in mind for any writing they are required to do.

We don't wish to suggest that a project should be so tightly structured by the teacher that it is impossible for any child to get lost on the way; where there is no possibility at all of error there are very limited opportunities for learning. What the teacher needs to be aware of is a range of interconnected lines of development which a project may take. This requires a bit more preparation and anticipation than, perhaps, teachers believe they have time for but the dividends make it well worth while. Given that project work demands considerable intellectual confidence on the part of the teacher plus an abundance of appropriate resources in the classroom the computer has already proved a significant aid to the management of classroom projects. It is not fanciful to compare Ph.D. students with a youngster about to compile, for example, a booklet reviewing changes in British Transport. Both need a sufficiently defined area to work in (a title, if you like); both need to ask themselves some questions at the outset in order to know if there are any answers in the mass of information they will inevitably collect; both need supervision from a tutor with whom they can sharpen up their ideas and formulate each new stage of the project.

Below is an example of a project in which the computer played a helpful though relatively minor role. What is demonstrated most effectively, however, is the pre-eminent importance of teacher supervision.

## A HISTORY PROJECT

The aim of the project was to investigate how the role of the English monarch has changed over 1000 years. This may seem a huge undertaking at first glance but the focus on specific kings and queens helps the children to understand something of the passage of time whilst giving them a personal life story or a series of life stories to concentrate on.

The children were introduced to the project by being asked to consider the fact that, although in 1066 William of Normandy was powerful enough to mobilise an army and invade Britain, there seems to be no evidence that Elizabeth II has a similar personal power. The reasons for this were discussed and the conclusion drawn that the present day role of the English Monarch has changed dramatically since the reign of William 1. It was considered that this shift of role could not have been a sudden one but would have been gradual and that we would try to trace and find the reasons behind this change. Since a period of 1000 years is extremely difficult for children to conceive they were shown in the first instance a complete chronological list of the kings and queens of England and their attention was then drawn particularly to six of them:

William I
Henry VIII
Elizabeth I
Charles I
Victoria
Elizabeth II

The children were divided into groups of fours and sixes and each group opted to base its research on one of the above monarchs. The work would consist of four pieces of writing each with an illustration and one large painting or model to be made near the completion of the work. The four essays would have the following titles:

- The Life of the Monarch.
- Important Events Involving the Monarch.
- The Life-Style of a Rich Person.
- The Life-Style of a Poor Person.

Working to this pattern made possible direct comparison between the different reigns and usefully divided up a large task into smaller, more easily managed units. It also meant that the children were aware of the individual aims of each piece of work as well as the overall aim of the project and were in a position to assess the relevance of any seemingly useful piece of information discovered during the course of their research.

As the work proceeded children shared the information they had discovered and were soon making comparisons between different social conditions. They discussed the significance of individual events and were sometimes able to help each other with new perspectives and with information from different sources. What was happening, in effect, was that pupils were collectively engaged in putting together a jigsaw puzzle. Each group made a display of its findings and completed written accounts, all of which enabled the children to begin to see what a historical period of 1000 years might look like. Once a framework of this kind has been constructed children are then free to introduce or follow up as much 'irrelevant' information as time would allow without losing sight of the overall project.

At this stage it was possible to consider how the computer might be used as an aid to or an extension of the project. By means of the program ELECTRONIC NEWS, a teletext emulator, pupils were introduced to another way of using and displaying their information.

## ELECTRONIC NEWS

ELECTRONIC NEWS allows the user to prepare, edit and display information in the form of 'electronic pages' on the monitor screen. The format is similar to that of the Ceefax and Oracle services. EDFAX and MIKEFAX are two other telextext emulators but with more facilities and a greater degree of sophistication than ELECTRONIC NEWS.

ELECTRONIC NEWS is in two parts: the first part enables pages to be created and then saved as files, or enables existing files to be altered and resaved; part two of the program loads in any files created using part one and displays them either from a menu or as a series of pages looped together and displayed for a period of time specified by the user.

In the history project under discussion the program was used to provide another form of display alongside other forms such as hand-written pieces of work, illustrations and paintings.

As will be appreciated a program of this type could be integrated into any project being studied. It will display any work undertaken and will also provide the basis for an additional project (producing a class electronic newspaper or a school bulletin board, for example).

While teletext emulators do enable the computer to provide a new and interesting dimension it must be admitted that this does not represent a vital contribution to the work. There are, however, programs available which allow pupils to undertake projects which would otherwise be impossible or extremely difficult without the use of a computer. FRONT PAGE, DIET and FACTFILE offer the teacher valuable assistance here and will be discussed in turn.

FRONT PAGE is a self-contained program which offers a useful tool for writing in a particular format; DIET is a simulation which provides a frame of reference for investigating personal information collected by the users; FACTFILE is an elementary database which can nevertheless be used in a variety of interesting ways.

## FRONT PAGE

FRONT PAGE is a newspaper front page emulator in the same way as ELECTRONIC NEWS is a teletext emulator. Published by MAPE the program allows the user to produce a realistic facsimile of a front page and to specify everything printed on it from the name of the newspaper to an advertisement at the foot of the page.

Operating the program is simple. The user is prompted to type in each element of the page beginning with the name of the newspaper, date of publication and price. The operator is then given the opportunity to type in his story and to draw a picture although this latter activity is difficult to perform in a convincing manner. Finally, the user is asked to type in an advertisement after which the whole page is printed out in a most satisfying way using an attached Epson-type printer. Our one criticism of the program is that, although the program will print as many copies as is desired, there is no facility for saving the newspaper data as a file on disc or for calling it up and reprinting it at a later date. There is some indication that a version which does just this is now available.

This program provides a powerful tool which will generate many ideas for its application. The production of a class newspaper, for instance, would gain immeasurably from a program which printed out creditable newspaper copy. This facility could also provide an avenue for reports of school events, accounts of class outings, advertisements for school productions and the book-shop, notices announcing visiting speakers and exhibitions, a swap-shop and indeed all the features you would expect to find in a local or national newspaper.

What starts off as learning how to use an emulator for a specific display purpose arising out of a project, can, in fact, turn into the real thing in which pupils are writing and using the program to satisfy their own interests and to accomplish wants and needs in their own everyday lives.

### FRONT PAGE in Use

When faced with a program of the calibre of FRONT PAGE it is tempting to base a whole project on its various applications. Doing this, however, may incline the exercise towards a more shallow approach than the program deserves; far better, perhaps, to integrate it into a larger project to which the program can give a new dimension. Consider, for instance, a project undertaken by a group of eleven-year-old children in which they imagined themselves to have been present at some famous historical event. They were asked to write a newspaper report giving a contemporary account of the event. Whilst this idea may not be new the facility to print a convincing copy of the report significantly increases interest and motivation. Not only that but the use of such a modern piece of technology seems to spark off rather more historical imagination than is usually achieved when primary school children are asked to do this kind of activity.

The project began with the provision of small portraits of famous people each with an inset illustration of a famous event in which that person played a significant part. The children's task was to discover for themselves by whatever means available the identity of the person in the portrait. This they did using a combination of inspired guesswork, careful scrutiny of the portrait and prolonged scouring of history books. Surprisingly, the initial problem was solved in a very short time.

The next task was to discover some information about the life of a given person and, in particular to discover why he or she was considered to be famous. In the course of this study certain central events were discovered and it was suggested to the children that one of these would provide an ideal subject for a newspaper report.

Next, a study was made of current newspapers and facsimiles of some newspaper front pages which reported famous events from the past such as the assassination of President Kennedy, Lindbergh's flight across the Atlantic and the first moon-landing. It became evident from this study that the writers of these reports adopted a consistent format and style of writing along the following lines:

- The headline proclaimed the crux of the story as dramatically as possible and in the minimum number of words.
- The first paragraph of the piece expanded the headline story by giving greater detail.
- The second paragraph of the report usually contained interviews with eye-witnesses or interested parties.

The children were asked to write their own reports in the form and style outlined above and in accordance with the requirements of the FRONT PAGE program.

- A newpaper name was required and, since no recognisable newspaper existed at the time of many events under consideration, this gave the children an opportunity to invent a convincing and fitting title for their publication.
- The date of publication was needed and, since newspaper reports are usually printed a day or so following an event, this needed careful research and consideration. Some reports of events would not

Figure 4.I: 'King's Head Rolls at Cromwell's Feet'. FRONT PAGE.

# The Puritan's Post

1p

31st January 1649

## King's Head Rolls at Cromwell's Feet

King Charles was hustled out to Whitehall the place of his execution. His last words were, "I fear not death; death is not terrible to me, I bless my God that I am prepared before I am executed".

When the executioner held up the severed head a great groan burst from the crowd. We interviewed an eye-witness who said, "It was such a groan as I never heard before and desire I may never hear again. "

Charles the first was the King of Great Britain and Ireland. He was the second son of King James the fourth of Scotland and he leaves one son, also Charles.

The Executioner Holds Up the King's Head.

Figure 4.2: 'Mad Dash From Wolf'. FRONT PAGE.

CHINNY-CHIN EXPRESS 1p

13th January 1886

Mad Dash from Wolf

Yesterday the criminal Wolf, commonly known as Blackeye, tried to murder the three little pigs from 12, Pigsty Cottage. The wolf evidently followed the three pigs to their homes.

The wolf viciously killed baby pig and master pig but the third pig was older and wiser and managed to tempt the wolf to come down the chimney into a boiling pot of soup.

The criminal wolf is finally dead and we can rest in peace.

We interviewed the surviving pig who wasn't a bit upset by the loss of his brothers. He said, "Life is like that."

The Criminal Wolf

BUY DANISH BACON

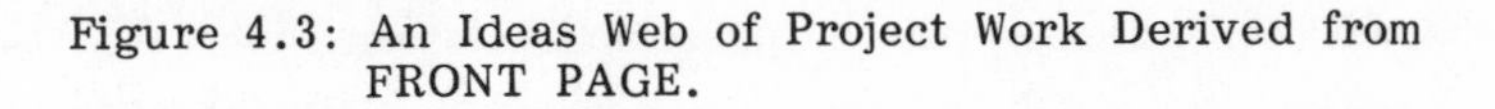

Figure 4.3: An Ideas Web of Project Work Derived from FRONT PAGE.

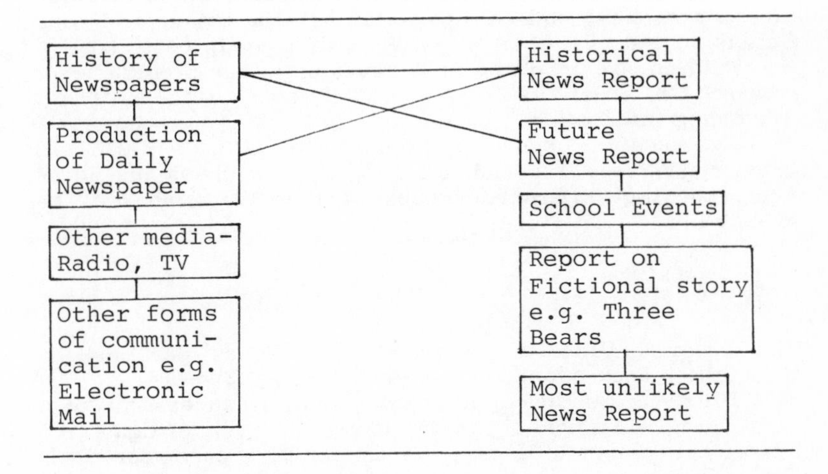


fit into this style and needed special treatment - for instance, the discovery of the deaths of those in Scott's expedition to the South Pole was not made until some months after the event.

- A single line advertisement to be printed at the bottom of the page was required by the program. Contemporary advertisements for reports concerning events which occurred in the Victorian age and after were comparatively easy to find; reports from earlier times gave children imaginative latitude and cause for much hilarity. One group of children, for instance, who had written their report about the execution of Charles I ended by imploring their readers to 'BUY WILKINSON SWORDS'!

Only when these considerable demands upon the children's writing had been fulfilled was the piece ready to be typed into the computer. Since the children had invested much time and effort into producing their work it is probably not surprising that the typing was performed with extreme care. In practice, however, it is usually quite simple to resolve any mistakes as the program behaves as a dedicated word-processor incorporating a useful deletion facility.

The activities described above are beneficial to the children in a number of ways. Consider, for instance, the fact that a children working on FRONT PAGE assume the role of a newspaper reporter and adopt what they think is a suitable style of writing. At the same time the children are constrained to write within a prescribed format and with specific and well-understood aims. Working together the children are involved in productive discussion which demands careful monitoring and editing of the material being produced. This is an example of collaborative writing at its best. Lastly, the children are involved in a finely-focussed programme of research in order to back up their story with sufficient convincing information.

Examples of print-outs produced by FRONT PAGE are given in Figures 4.1 and 4.2. Figure 4.3 shows an 'ideas web', showing different avenues of thought which may be explored.

## DIET

The program DIET is published by MEP as part of the Microprimer Pack supplied to English Primary Schools.

DIET, as mentioned in Chapter One, is an example of a model program which allows an individual to investigate the nutritional content of a complete diet or of a particular meal. The program will translate and display a given weight of a particular food into its constituent amounts of protein, carbohydrate, fat, fibre and energy.

The program will also display, in graph form, the dietary needs, broken down into the same constituents described above, of an average male or female up to the age of 35. This graph of daily needs will be retained on the screen. When an individual's consumption of food for one day is inputted it will be displayed on the same graph and a comparison of dietary needs against consumption can be made. An example of such a graph is given in Figure 4.4.

The value of this program for the study of biology in the secondary school can be readily appreciated. It is reputed to have been designed for a mainframe computer used by college students. With the advent of this program it is now possible for primary and secondary school children to study the question of diet in far more specific ways than had hitherto been possible in general biology lessons. DIET provides us with a tool which enables children to discover for themselves the suitability of what they eat. It also provides them with the information necessary, if they so wish, to change their existing diet to a more healthy one.

Accordingly, a project was designed which would enable children to study the value of different foods to the human body and which used the program DIET as an investigative tool. The overall title of the project was 'Food as Fuel'.

### Food as Fuel

This work involved a group of eleven-year-olds and began

Figure 4.4: An Example of a Graph Showing the Dietary Needs of an Eleven-year-old Girl and the Effects of the Favourite Diet. DIET.

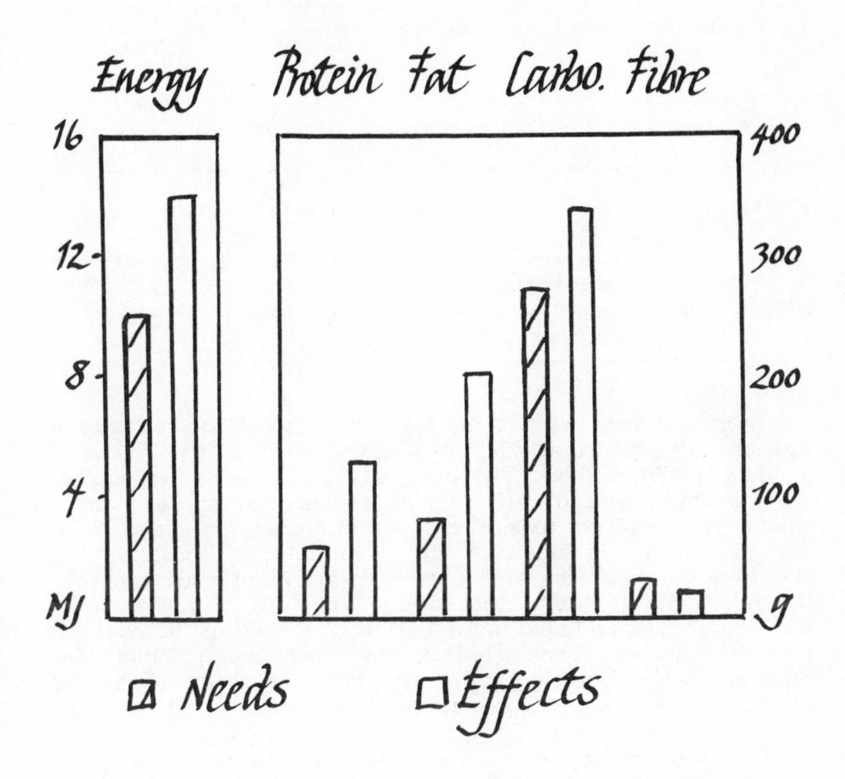


with the question 'What would you like to eat, everyday?' and ended with the question 'What ought you to eat, everyday?'.

The children were first engaged in a discussion concerning their favourite foods. They were asked how often they ate them and why they liked these particular foods. When asked if any foods were 'better' for them than other foods the children cited various types of fruit and vegetables. Upon being asked if any foods were 'bad' for them they universally identified foods high in sugar - chocolate, sweets, etc. - as being responsible for tooth decay. Thus the children did have some idea of the effects on the body of different diets.

Working in groups of four or five the children constructed a list of a day's meals containing the foods they would like to eat if given a free choice. The menus varied considerably although most contained chips and ice-cream and all were, nutritionally speaking, disastrous! A class menu was agreed by voting and was written upon the blackboard. This menu is shown in Figure 4.5.

Figure 4.5: The Children's Menu of Favourite Foods.

| | |
|---|---|
| BREAKFAST | Cup of tea, cornflakes, pizza, toast, bacon, egg, tomato, sausage. |
| LUNCH | Chicken, chips, baked-beans, strawberries and cream. |
| DINNER | Steak, chips, egg, carrots, cake, ice-cream, crackers. |

The children were then introduced to DIET and shown how the program could help to assess the nutritional value of a day's intake of food. The program was requested to display the dietary needs of an average eleven-year-old girl after which the children took turns at inputting the class menu agreed earlier. Included in the documentation accompanying the program is a list of foods and associated code numbers which are inputted into the computer instead of the name of the food; also included is a list of the weights of average portions of each food listed in the class menu. Thus, for example, boiled potatoes appear in the list as code number 37 of which, we are informed, 180g represents an average portion.

As each amount of food contained in the diet was typed into the computer the nutritional make-up was calculated by the program and displayed in figures. This amount was added to the graphical representation shown on the screen adjacent to one showing the dietary needs. The children watched in mounting horror as the values of the menu very soon equalled those prescribed and very quickly overtook the prescribed figures finally reaching those shown in Figure 4.4.

The display showed that the diet contained excessive amounts of carbohydrate, protein, fibre, fat and energy but since the children had little idea of the meaning of these terms they did not know whether or not this was desirable. Dictionary definitions were simplified so that the children understood the following:

- Energy is the fuel which powers the human body.
- Carbohydrates and fats represent concentrated stores of body energy.

- Proteins provide materials with which the body can repair and rebuild itself.
- Fibre makes a considerable contribution to the efficiency with which the body can process food and eliminate its wastes.

The question of the desirability of these excessive amounts, however, remained unanswered until it was pointed out to the children that a diet having too great a content of carbohydrate and fat would result in obesity and that too much protein and too little fibre content in the diet are thought to contribute towards certain diseases.

Armed with this information the children concluded that the day's menu containing all the foods they would like to eat was decidedly unhealthy and would require extreme modification. They also showed an interest in performing a similar assessment of their usual daily diet and it was decided that this would be attempted.

The children were required to choose either the Saturday or Sunday of the following weekend and on that day were to weigh everything they ate and note this down on a form supplied for the purpose. Teachers who have already tried something along these lines know that parents' reactions will not be entirely favourable and also know what risks they run! In the event only one child was forbidden by his parents to weigh the amounts of food and, consequently, had to sacrifice some accuracy by using the weights given in the documentation for average portions. Contrast this with another child who, away from home for the weekend, nevertheless took scales with her and carried out the whole operation in a caravan.

The children returned to school on the Monday with their recorded daily intakes of food, a list of various foods and a selection of empty food wrappers. Using DIET the former contents of these wrappers were discovered to have high concentrations of protein, fat, carbohydrate or fibre. The wrappers were incorporated into wall displays to illustrate information and to make it readily accessible.

The children wrote reports to explain the methods which had been adopted and to give the reasoning behind them. At the same time the children typed the details of their day's food consumptions into the computer, noted the results given and made copies of the graph showing dietary needs alongside the consumption. They analysed the results by looking at each dietary component and comparing consumption with needs. Finally, they were asked to make suggestions of how they could improve or balance their diets.

It was made clear to the children that the data they had obtained were not to be taken too literally and represented merely an indication of trends. A more reliable account of the suitability of their diets could only be obtained by monitoring

Figure 4.6: An Ideas Web for the Project 'Food as Fuel'.

Initial question: What would you LIKE to eat everyday?

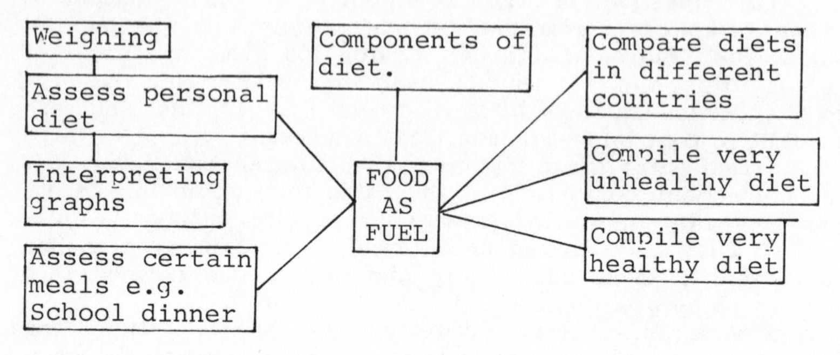


Final question: What OUGHT you to eat everyday?

their consumption over a greater period of time and using a more accurate tool than DIET.

The procedures outlined above represent only part of the activities undertaken in the 'Food as Fuel' project. An 'Ideas Web' upon which the project was based is reproduced in Figure 4.6 and shows ideas stemming from the central theme. Some of these ideas were incorporated in the study and others would have proved equally fertile if time had permitted them to be explored.

During this project the children used a variety of skills including for example, the mathematical skills of accurate weighing and of making and interpreting graphs. Scientific skills used included recording and analysing data. The language development which can take place in a project such as this will be self-evident: the learning of new words e.g. 'carbohydrate' and 'protein'; the syntax of describing comparisons and observing contrasts; the language and thought of scientific analysis; the writing and recording of accurate information.

Although DIET facilitates the study of an otherwise difficult subject it is a specific tool with restricted uses. So-called 'open' programs, which can be used in a wider range of fields are likely to become more common in project-based work. One particularly interesting program developed by Geoff Chadwick of North Cheshire College is AMAZING which asks users to make a series of connections in their own chosen topic. The 'connections' grow into a web of phenomena and ideas associated with a particular theme or subject and a loop device enables the user periodically to jump out of the series or trains of connections into a new set of links.

## DATABASES

The use of databases in the primary classroom crept in early alongside the newly-introduced personal computers and their use was justified at the time by reference to the desirability of using new technology and of stimulating computer-awareness. Not surprisingly, these early programs were usually based upon commercial designs, these being the only pattern available. As far as primary schools were concerned they were often clumsy and difficult to use. Luckily, it was not long before teachers themselves made it their business to produce databases designed for primary-age children and which contained minimum jargon and maximum user-friendliness. One such example is FACTFILE.

FACTFILE is a deceptively simple database program which will allow children to input a file composed of a number of items along with associated information under further headings from one to ten. Upon completion, the file can be saved on tape or disc to be reloaded at a later date. The user can look at an individual file, inspect all of the files consecutively or can interrogate the program by specifying his exact requirements within a number of headings and allowing the program to search and find the required data.

Figure 4.7: A File of Weather Words Used With FACTFILE.

| FILENAME<br>Weather | | ITEM<br>Descriptions | | | |
|---|---|---|---|---|---|
| No. | Description | Cold? | Wet? | Misty? | Windy? |
| 1 | snowing | yes | yes | no | no |
| 2 | freezing | yes | no | no | no |
| 3 | bleak | yes | no | no | yes |
| 4 | warm | no | no | no | no |
| 5 | moist | no | yes | yes | no |
| 6 | foggy | yes | yes | yes | no |
| 7 | fresh | no | no | no | yes |
| 8 | raining | no | yes | no | no |
| 9 | stormy | no | yes | no | yes |
| 10 | arctic | yes | yes | no | yes |

Database programs are good examples of the computer being used as a tool and, because of their content-free nature, can be introduced into a great number of projects. Figure 4.7, for example, illustrates part of a file amassed by a class of eight-year-olds. The children had been discussing the Winter weather and had found that weather descriptions such a 'freezing' and 'frosty', far from being the generalisations they are often assumed to be, were actually very specific descriptions of temperature which could not be used interchangeably without some alteration of meaning.

The children, working in small groups, were encouraged to suggest new descriptions of the weather and, as they determined its precise characteristics, to fill in a grid similar to the one shown. This operation, although often a simple one, sometimes was the cause of animated discussion. When the children considered, for example, the word 'snowing' they decided it obviously meant 'cold and wet' but did not necessarily mean 'windy'. It is often, however, difficult to see very far when it is snowing and the children wondered if this indicated that the weather was 'misty'. They eventually decided that 'misty' implied 'moisture' or 'wetness', as they called it, would be hanging in the air and that, since 'snowing' meant that 'frozen water and air mixed' was falling through the air, they concluded that the entry under 'Misty?' should be 'no'. This kind of attention paid to a single word is most impressive.

As the children's contributions increased in number they were added to a master list and inputted into FACTFILE. This file could now be used in a variety of ways:

- as a dictionary; by requesting to look at a file and at one of the descriptions the program will respond with a definition of the word asked for.
- as a thesaurus; by requesting the program, for instance, to search for words which have 'yes' as their entry under 'Wet?', a list of all of the words meaning wet contained in the file will be displayed.
- as a comparison tool; by interrogating the program under a number of headings words with similar entries can be compared to discover what differences, if any, there are between them e.g. notice that 'raining' and 'stormy' have the same entries under three headings yet only differ on their 'Windy?' entry.

It is interesting to reflect that, whilst dictionaries and thesauri have existed for many years, the invention of a tool which allows comparison of the differences as well as the similarities in the meaning of words has had to wait for the invention of the computer.

FACTFILE also has many applications for projects in which large amounts of data are being used as in the next example.

Estate

This project was conceived by Ernie Tarn of Lacey Green Primary School, Wilmslow, who operated it with a class of ten-year-olds.

The children had been discussing logic in mathematics with special reference to attributes and binary work. During this work the children had filled in attribute cards referring to themselves and containing questions to which the only answers could be 'yes' or 'no'. They had used a mechanical sorting process to investigate the information stored in the cards based on a method originally used by early computers in which cards are prepared with holes adjacent to the questions being asked; if the answer to any question is a 'yes' the hole is left intact; however, if the answer is a 'no' the hole is cut into a slot. To remove all those cards for which the answer to any particular question is 'yes' is a simple matter of inserting a thin rod through these slots and pulling them from the pack.

It was first explained to the children that many organisations are using the sorting abilities of a database program to improve the running of their companies. Estate agents, for instance, have computers in their offices and use them to store information about the houses they wish to sell. The idea of houses having attributes proved intriguing and was chosen as a topic worthy of further investigation. Eight attributes were selected and a vocabulary established which would enable information to be accessed once it had been put into FACTFILE. Some of these attributes and vocabulary are illustrated in Figure 4.8.

Figure 4.8: Attributes and Vocabulary for Houses for Use With FACTFILE

| STYLE | TYPE | PRICE | BEDS | GARAGE | LOCATION |
|---|---|---|---|---|---|
| house<br>bungalow<br>cottage | detached<br>semi<br>terraced | 9500<br>to<br>49000 | 1<br>to<br>5 | yes<br>no | near shops<br>not near shops |

Details of houses were obtained from actual estate agents and the children sifted through this information. Using the vocabulary shown in Figure 4.8 they completed a file card for each house. The information was typed into the FACTFILE program and the children were then able to use its facilities to solve comparatively easy problems such as finding all the semi-detached houses with garages or all houses within specified price bands.

As the work progressed the children were encouraged to take from FACTFILE information about a particular house and to make their own estate agent's information sheets. This involved children in:

- making inferrences from the raw information at their disposal
- writing advertisements
- drawing a picture of the property and using their judgement to estimate what sort of family the house would suit.

An example of one such information sheet is reproduced in Figure 4.9.

Conversely, the children were asked to suppose themselves to be members of a family which required a particular kind of house. They were then asked to interrogate FACTFILE and find suitable accomodation for their 'family'. It was during this work that role-play began to enter into the project. The children set up an estate agent's office with receptionist and agent; other children acted as would-be sellers and buyers, visiting the office with various requirements. Details of houses for sale were taken by the estate agent and put into the computer. Hopeful buyers discussed their requirements with him, interrogated the file of houses and obtained copies of the particulars of the ones which were thought to be suitable.

This work was further extended by setting up a file of information about cars based upon the Police National Computer. They also constructed a file of holidays such as a travel agent might use. As this work progressed an 'electronic village' was brought into existence centring on police station, travel agents and estate agents with consequent opportunities for more role-play. The children wrote stories and plays revolving around the life of the village. Cars, for instance, were involved in accidents at which witnesses saw only part of a registration plate. Searches using the car file helped to reveal which vehicles might have been involved. Subsequent investigations necessitated visits to homes for checking alibis. All the features traditionally found in a fictional 'whodunnit' began to emerge!

The use of FACTFILE during the course of this project involved children in using many different but allied skills. Dictionaries, encyclopaedias and source books must first be consulted for the initial raw material which then has to be sorted, systematically organised and prepared for inclusion

Figure 4.9: A Reproduction of a Child's Estate Agent's Information Sheet. FACTFILE.

Brook Vale and Partners

34 Layby Hill, Old Town.

| Style | House |
|---|---|
| Type | Detatched |
| Price | £31,000 |
| Beds | 3 |
| Garage | Yes |
| Location | Near Shops |
| Develop-ment | Old Town |
| Tel. No. | 718327 |

in the database. Interrogating the database requires a familiarity with the general vocabulary of the database and the specific vocabulary of the particular material being used. Knowing how to ask the program to search involves the use of a number of language skills as does the ability to interpret the information yielded and to draw conclusions from that information.

## SOME REFLECTIONS

Project-based work is, in most primary schools, an important way of working and, if undertaken with care and with clearly defined aims, can contribute significantly to the development of children's skills in many areas of language and learning. To include the use of a computer in this style of working is becoming a natural extension for many teachers.

There is no doubt that, although the teletext emulator program does make a novel addition to the repertoire of display media, the history project described earlier could have been undertaken without its use and would have suffered little as a result. However, the newspaper project using FRONT PAGE demostrated that, although a handwritten newspaper could have been produced without the aid of the computer, the facility to produce a convincing facsimile enhanced the quality of the children's experience and contributed greatly to the authenticity of the project.

Similarly the exclusion of the program DIET from the Food as Fuel project would have left a significant gap. Having a mechanism with which one's own diet can be analysed gives the project a uniquely personal element. Far too many projects in the past have been long on information and short on relevance.

The two projects which involved the use of FACTFILE could have been undertaken without using a computer database but its presence served not only as an instrument but as a catalyst for additional language exploration. In one case the children found a way of ranging through a set of words for describing weather which yielded an unanticipated layer of information. In the second case the computer itself suggested the context and provided detailed information for highly imaginative role-play.

The question of more developed uses of databases in the primary school and of using more sophisticated databases e.g. SUPASTORE (ESM 1986) is a difficult one because of the complexity of thought and operation involved. One of the most common arguments for the use of databases is that they familiarise children with the use of databases which seems a peculiarly circular argument. Undoubtably databases do stimulate and can act as a catalyst for language development. It is essential though that children should use databases for real purposes connected with things they are actually learning about or experiencing at the time. If not there is a danger that children will simply be pushed through a series of procedural exercises thought of as particularly appropriate training for the age of information technology but lacking any generalisable intellectual value.

Chapter Five

# WULFSTAN'S WORDHOARD

WULFSTAN'S WORDHOARD is a computer program for people who don't like computers. Through the program the computer renounces its role as a computer and pretends to be merely an instrument of communication between the user and an invented character called Wulfstan. The program is thus extremely user-friendly although it has been suggested that the grouchy and rather short-tempered Wulfstan is, if anything, user-hostile, though in an entertaining way.

One way of using WULFSTAN'S WORDHOARD is to make it the imaginative core of a language project, in which the activities initiated by the program may be directed or extended to suit the particular interests and purposes of the children and teacher using it. Although the program is of the project-based type, discussed elsewhere, WORDHOARD is, at present, unique in its presentation and it has been accorded a chapter of its own.

## THE PROGRAM

WULFSTAN'S WORDHOARD is published by ESM and was written during a Curriculum Development Project undertaken by the Cheshire Language Centre at North Cheshire College and financed by MEP. It is designed for nine to eleven-year-olds.

'Wordhoard' is an Anglo-Saxon word for 'language' and the program invites children to become a part of a scenario in which they communicate with Wulfstan who is an imaginary Anglo-Saxon story-teller from the tenth century. In some respects the program has the look of a fantasy or adventure game but instead of children finding strange creatures to kill, they are given opportunities to tell stories and give information about their own life and times in exchange for Anglo-Saxon lore from Wulfstan. He asks them to become his apprentices and to perform various language tasks in order, eventually, to become master wordsmiths in their own right. The children undertake their apprenticeships in groups of two or three and Wulfstan gives each of these groups a 'stone name', e.g. Diamond or Amethyst. He records the names of the individual members of the groups (by setting up a file of the names on disc) so that, at any stage, he can 'remember' them and 'recollect' which tasks have been completed by each group.

The program is designed to be used over a period of weeks during which the children take part in a number of language activities initiated both by the program and by their teacher. This core of work will provide a spring-board for work in other areas, such as art and craft, in true project-based tradition.

The three tasks completed by the children as part of their apprenticeships require three different kinds of writing within three language areas:

- Factual description of familiar objects.
- Imaginative descriptions developed into a narrative.
- Poetry-writing.

Each task is presented in two parts, the first initiating a comparatively simple activity, the second developing it further and requiring the children to use the work produced for the first part. The program is designed to develop different kinds of descriptive skills and to encourage the children to write stories and poetry whilst consciously using these skills. Figure 5.1 illustrates a way in which these activities may be seen to be connected.

As the core of a scheme for project-based work, WORDHOARD could be the launching point of any number of other writing activities e.g. a description and biography of a person; a story combining Anglo-Saxons with modern times to set the scene for interesting or amusing anachronisms (there is a story, 'Who Taught Them to Ride Motorbikes?' included in the pack and which is based on this theme). There are also many opportunities for illustrating ideas and events. The children can make paintings, for example, of such subjects as 'The Tribe of Wulfstan' or 'An Anglo-Saxon Village'. Maps and scenes inspired by the children's own stories as well as by ancient tales such as Beowulf may also be included. The children whose experiences of WORDHOARD are described in this chapter produced hand-made books sewn, bound and decorated with lino prints which they had designed themselves and which were inspired by things Anglo-Saxon. Into these books the children wrote copies of all the work done by a particular group. The program is designed so that it initiates activities which the children do away from the computer only returning to it when a task has been completed.

WULFSTAN'S WORDHOARD is a project pack rather than just a computer program and consists of

Figure 5.1: Language Activities Initiated by WORDHOARD.

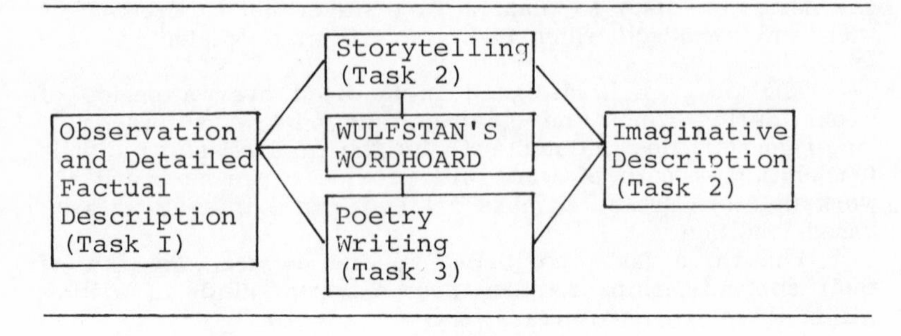


- Eight picture cards of maps and characters (with no restrictions on copying).
- A classroom poster of 'The Great Hall'.
- A story book, 'Who Taught Them to Ride Motorbikes?'.
- A teachers' handbook of information and suggestions.
- The program disc.

A project based on WORDHOARD could take many different forms depending on the requirements and interests of the teacher. A possible project is illustrated by the Ideas Web shown in Figure 5.2.

Using the Program

The program begins by displaying first the logo representing the WORDHOARD and then another, suggesting a spinning cube. The children are given greetings from Wulfstan the Wordhoarder who pompously introduces himself as a traveller and teller of tales. He alludes to the mysterious 'crystal cube' by which he speaks 'across the centuries' but the children are left to form their own conclusions as to his exact identity. They usually decide in the end that he is either an Anglo-Saxon or a Viking. Wulfstan further expounds on the power of words and stories and invites the children to become apprentice wordsmiths, in which capacity, he informs them, they will acquire a mastery of language if they successfully complete three tasks. In performing the tasks children add their words, ideas and stories to Wulfstan's Wordhoard and he, in exchange, adds to their wordhoards.

The children 'sign' a contract with Wulfstan by typing their names into the computer. The monitor screen displays a scroll which is headed 'Apprentices' underneath which each child's name appears written in suitably archaic script. After

Figure 5.2: Ideas Web of a Possible Project Using WORDHOARD.

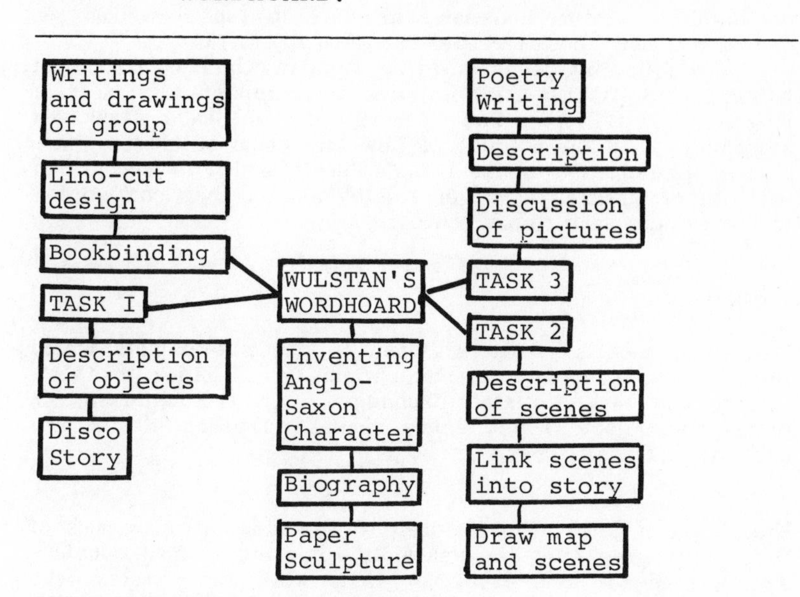


this each group of children is given the code name of a type of stone which is used to identify them whenever they return to the computer. The program keeps a record of the progress of each group which can be inspected by the teacher at any time and which can also be printed out on an Epson-type printer if one is available. The groups can contain up to three children and the program will manage up to 20 groups after which number it will re-issue earlier stone names providing that those groups have completed their three tasks.

A 'Jumper' option is also available which allows any of the tasks to be undertaken without reference to group names or a group's progress. This option could be used by the teacher to preview each task in order to become familiar with it, or the feature may be used if a group, perhaps, has misunderstood the requirements of a particular task and needs to repeat it.

During each of the tasks the children are required to fill in pages which they will have already prepared. These pages could be loose sheets of paper or the pages of a notebook. In the project described in this chapter the children designed and made their own books using the traditional bookbinding skills of stitching, laminating and binding. The covers were decorated using prints of their own design. This activity was seen as an integral part of the project linking traditional skills with modern technology. For a more detailed account of bookbinding, its methods and its uses in the classroom see one of the many books written on the subject.(1)

The following pages describe ways in which each task of WULFSTAN'S WORDHOARD initiates and supports a variety of language activities. The description of each task is accompanied by an account of how one class of eleven-year-olds completed each of the tasks. There is also an account of how other activities were generated and how they contributed to the project as a whole.

## TASK 1

This first task asks the children to describe objects which they use in everyday life and which are familiar to them. During the task Wulfstan exchanges with the children his names for objects which serve similar purposes in his own everyday life and times.

Task 1, Part 1
Wulfstan introduces the children to the idea of the names of things changing over the years by referring to an example - asking them, in one case, for their word for someone who sings and volunteering the name 'bard' in exchange. The children are then asked to look at the picture of The Great Hall and at the workcard containing a simplified picture of the same scene on which some objects have been numbered. Wulfstan asks the children to look carefully at these objects and to try to work out what they would be used for. When they have done this the children are asked to make a list of objects in their own homes which serve similar purposes to those in the picture of the Great Hall.

In Use. The children were introduced to the project by the teacher reading to them, rather enigmatically and with no explanation, the story 'Who Taught Them to Ride Motorbikes?' which is part of the package. The 'them' of the title are Anglo-Saxons and Vikings who have somehow invaded the twentieth centurey, pillaged the local Co-op and run riot in the play ground of a primary school. Discussion following this story concerned itself with the utter impossibility of these events, on the one hand, and with speculation on the other hand about the differences between then and now:

- Just what are the differences between a dragon and a helicopter?
- Who is Wulfstan and did he really exist?
- Why couldn't the people in the fish and chip shop

queue understand what the Anglo-Saxons had been saying?

These are just some of the intriguing questions raised. After this discussion the children were asked to form groups of twos and threes, to prepare pages in their personal books and to prepare the same pages in a book which was designated their 'group book'. Each group then approached the computer in turn and was 'introduced' to the project by Wulfstan himself in his own inimitable, slightly pompous way.

During their dialogue with Wulfstan each group used the poster of The Great Hall and workcard both of which became topics of much discussion. A mode of working was devised which was to become standard throughout the project and consisted of each child working initially alone and writing down his own list of names. When each child had completed this work the different sets of answers were discussed by each group during which those answers considered best were written in the group book. An example of this is reproduced in Figure 5.3.

The work was then discussed with the teacher who made sure that the children had fully understood what was required of them. Although the purposes of most objects are self-evident some, like the drawing of dried meat hanging from the roof of the great hall, may require an explanation. Drying meat was, for example, an old way of preserving food and children need to consider in what ways food is preserved in modern times.

With this work completed the groups took their information back to Wulfstan. In practice, however, the computer was not immediately available to the group and so the children were asked to work on another facet of the project - either binding their group book or working on an associated interest.

Figure 5.3: A List of Names of Objects for the Word Exchange

| My Word | Your Word |
|---|---|
| 1. | 1. Plate |
| 2. | 2. Cup |
| 3. | 3. Carpet |
| 4. | 4. Cooker |
| 5. | 5. Mattress |
| 6. | 6. Blankets |
| 7. | 7. Pan |
| 8. | 8. Tinned meat |
| 9. | 9. Hat |

One of the extra pieces of work the children were asked to do was to write a story based on the one read to them at the beginning of the project and concerned with the anachronisms which could occur should Anglo-Saxons suddenly find themselves transported into the modern day. The children were asked to discuss the idea as a group and then write their own ideas of what could happen if their local weekly disco should be invaded by Wulfstan's friends. An excerpt from one of these stories is reproduced in Figure 5.4.

Figure 5.4: An Excerpt from 'Anglo-Saxons at the Disco' by Katy.

---

We were just buying a drink at the counter when there was a sudden commotion at the door and a lot of banging and shouting. Then into the hall poured a group of funny men wearing clothes that looked OK for a fancy dress party. The hats had horns on and the men hd funny long beards. About five of them ran up to the deejay and started stamping on the stereo, pulling plugs out of the wiring and smashing lights to bits. Then a really strange one came up and pinched a can of coke, jumped around and then stopped. All of the men crowded around him as he pulled the top off the can. There was a loud bang and fizzy coke poured all over the place. This had a strange effect on the men. There was another commotion and they ran through the door, jumped on Sinclair mini cars and rode off acting as if they had never seen them before. They were on the wrong side of the road and wobbling everywhere. The Police arrived just as they left, late as usual.

---

Task 1, Part 2

At the beginning of Part Two of the task the computer interrogates each group of children to discover their group name. When this has been typed in, the program directs itself to the second part of Task 1.

The children are asked to make sure that they have their word-exchange table with them (Figure 5.3). The program then displays a similar table and asks the children to type in the words they have decided upon. As they do so, the names for the Anglo-Saxon objects shown in the the picture of the Great Hall also appear and direct comparison can be made between the lists. Figure 5.5 shows an example of what the complete table could look like. At no point is there any suggestion nor do the children infer that their words are 'wrong' because they are different from Wulfstan's. It is the difference which stimulates curiosity and promotes learning.

Figure 5.5: An Example of the Completed Word-Exchange Table.

| My Word | Your Word |
|---|---|
| 1. Trencher | 1. Plate |
| 2. Tumbler | 2. Cup |
| 3. Rushes | 3. Carpet |
| 4. Hearth | 4. Cooker |
| 5. Bed-place | 5. Mattress |
| 6. Wolfskin | 6. Blankets |
| 7. Cauldron | 7. Pan |
| 8. Dried meat | 8. Tinned meat |
| 9. Helmet | 9. Hat |

At the next stage the program displays only the Anglo-Saxon half of the table and offers the children an opportunity to discover more about any word by typing in its number. If this is done the information about an object is presented as a page upon which three questions are answered. Figure 5.6 is a reproduction of one of these information pages.

All descriptions of size used in this section are done without reference to units and use only comparisons to various parts of the body as in the example shown.

The children are invited to explore the information pages at their leisure, information being presented in each case as the answer to one of three questions. As will be appreciated, the answers to the three questions together furnish a sufficient description of an object to anyone unfamiliar with it.

Wulfstan now feigns ignorance of some of the objects from the children's list and specifically names three, chosen by the computer at random, which interest him. He asks the children to describe the objects by posing and answering the same three questions as in his examples. The children leave the computer in order to do so.

Figure 5.6: An Example of One of Wulfstan's Information Pages.

```
        A Trencher

What shape and size is it?
    A trencher is a little bigger than a man's head.
What is it made of?
    It is usually made of wood but sometimes of pewter.
What is it for?
    We serve our food from a trencher and eat off one.
```

Figure 5.7: Descriptions Given by Garnet Group.

---

First Word..Blanket

What shape and size is it?
A blanket can be square or rectangular. The blanket is also flat and just bigger than a man and in width as fat as one.
What is it made of?
A blanket is made from wool which comes from sheep.
What is it for?
A blanket is for keeping you warm in Winter and at night.

Second Word...Freezer

What shape and size is it?
It is shaped like a coffin and is about the height of a tall man and the width of a fat man.
What is it made of?
It is made of metal, plastic and rubber. Plastic is made from oil which is the juice from rotted down trees. Rubber is made from latex which is from a rubber tree.
What is it for?
It is to keep food cold and preserve it.

Third Word...Hat.

What shape and size is it?
It is the same shape as a helmet only it doesn't have horns.
What is it made of?
It is made of wool, cloth or straw.
What is it for?
It is for keeping your head warm.

---

In Use. The same mode of working as described in part one was used again. First, children worked separately on their descriptions and then came together as a group to discuss the various answers they had given. Each group eventually agreed upon its composite answers and these were written into group books. Figure 5.7 shows the answers agreed by one group.

Following this each member of the group was asked to prepare a picture of one of their objects and, underneath it, to write a description based upon the one previously supplied though, this time, omitting the questions. Once they begin to see the importance of communicating helpful information to Wulfstan their descriptions became much more thoughtful. An example of one of these descriptions is given in Figure 5.8.

Figure 5.8: An Example of a Description.

Microwave Oven

An oven is about as big as a door or as small as a cupboard. It is made of electrical appliances and metal. It is for cooking food in.

Further work undertaken by the children consisted of inventing a member of Wulfstan's Tribe. This was approached from a practical point of view, the children being asked to measure the size of a fellow group-member's head using a pencil as the unit of measurement. These sizes were transferred to a piece of white paper and used, along with direct comparison, to draw a realistically shaped face which was cut out and stuck to another piece of coloured paper. The children were then required, using paper-sculpture technique, to transform the face into a three-dimensional representation of the face of a member of Wulfstan's Tribe. When completed, it was necessary to name the individual with a convincing Anglo-Saxon name and to prepare a description of the individual, partly taken from the paper sculpture and partly taken from imagination. The children were also asked to write a convincing biography of their character and to include information concerning his or her family. Figure 5.9 reproduces part of one such biography.

All of the work initiated in or derived from Task 1 was written up in the group book. Where feasible, copies were made on paper and displayed on wall boards.

Figure 5.9: An Excerpt from 'Hebrese the Archer' by Nicky.

---

Hebrese was born in a small village in the south of England called Scotthaid. He was very adventurous from the age of two and at ten became the best runner. When he was sixteen the time came to try at the best archer competition. He practiced days and days on end. When the big day came he broke his leg but he still won and so became the village archer.

---

TASK 2

Task 2 builds upon the children's experience gained in Task 1 and extends some comparatively simple skills of factual description to more complex imaginative description.

Task 2, Part 1

Wulfstan's travel tales are a traditional blend of fact and fiction. He describes to the children how, when telling a story of one of his many journeys, he recalls the answers to three questions. The three questions are:

- What could I see there?
- What could I hear there?
- What might have happened there?

The children are then asked to look at one of the worksheets which contains a map showing some of the places visited by Wulfstan on his latest journey. He asks them to consider three places which can be found on the map:

- A sleepy wood
- A desolate hill
- A tumbling stream

Wulstan takes his first location, the sleepy wood, and gives the children possible answers to the three questions previously shown. He then presents them with the second location and, this time, gives an answer to the first question only. At the third location he again answers only the first question but also asks the children, as part of their second task, to write answers to the other two questions. They leave the computer to do so.

In Use. The children worked in the method that was becoming familiar to them. They first answered the questions individ-

Figure 5.10: Answers to the Location Questions Written by Bloodstone Group.

```
Location 1 - A sleepy wood

What might I see there?
     Fresh footprints in the ground.
What might I hear there?
     A deep rumble.
What might happen there?
     A wild boar might burst out of the undergrowth.

Location 2 - A desolate hill

What might I see there?
     A granite tower.
What might I hear there?
     A crumbling noise.
What might happen there?
     The granite tower might suddenly fall down.

Location 3 - A tumbling stream

What might I see there?
     A moored boat.
What might I hear there?
     A ghostly cry.
What might happen there?
     The boat might sink and a dragonship may appear.
```

ually before going on to discuss their different answers. Figure 5.10 reproduces the answers eventually agreed on by the members of Bloodstone Group.

Task 2, Part 2

The children next return to the computer armed with answers similar to those shown above and are, once again, greeted by Wulfstan. He asks them to type in the answers they have written for one of the locations and when they have done so suggests that they now turn these incidents into the episodes of a journey across the country shown on the map.

In Use. It was suggested to the children that they should first make drawings showing the scenes at the locations so that they could refer to them for their factual and imaginative descriptions. They were also asked to imagine that it was not as themselves that they were going on the journey but as the Anglo-Saxon characters they had invented as part of Task 1. They were further required to suggest some convincing explanation why these characters were making their journey. Each member of the group took responsibility for an episode or chapter of the story which would be centred around one of the three locations.

It was suggested to the children that the 'shape' of the story should follow closely the plan shown in Figure 5.11.

Figure 5.11: A Plan for a Story About a Journey.

---

Introduction: characters, reason for journey, preparations.

Day 1: early rising, travelling, the sleepy wood, adventure and escape, camp for night.

Day 2: rising, travelling, the desolate hill, adventure and escape, camp for night.

Day 3: rising, travelling, a tumbling stream, adventure and escape, journey's end.

---

When the children had completed a first draft of their complete story they were asked to examine their own episodes and to use a dictionary to check any spellings they were unsure about. The children were then asked to read aloud to the rest of the group an episode written by another member of the group. As they did so, everyone listened to the story for any parts which did not seem to make sense or which did not sound quite right. Following this the group made revisions, incorporated new ideas and, in effect, redrafted the original writing. When this was done to everyone's satisfaction, including the teacher's, the story was written out in final form in the group book and also on paper for wall display. The story written by Bloodstone Group is reproduced in its entirety in Figure 5.12.

An examination of the story reveals clearly the episodes which the group had originally decided upon in their answers shown in Figure 5.10. Similarly, the structure shown in Figure 5.11 is also discernible. These two planning aids had considerable influence upon the story, giving the children an understanding of where their story-telling is taking them and what its conclusion might be.

This, of course, is by no means the end of the story but rather, so far as the writing is concerned, a new starting point. Discussion with the children soon brought out the importance of attention to detail in story-telling:

- Wouldn't it be better if they had some idea of where they were going?
- Couldn't they trick the boar somehow?
- The granite tower needs a lot more explanation.
- The tumbling stream would have to widen into a river eventually if it were to carry the Viking ship which appears at the end of the story.

These are the sort of questions and collaborative decisions that give rewriting a sense of purpose and direction. They do not detract from what has already been achieved imaginatively - the idea of a cow in tow, for example, is a nice touch while the Hobbit-like preoccupation with food and sleep is very natural. What the program seems to do, in practice, is to help children to weave the good bits into a satisfying story line.

## TASK 3

The third and final task of WULFSTAN'S WORDHOARD is to write a poem. The children, having completed the previous two tasks, will already have had considerable experience of factual and imaginative description which should provide them with a broad base from which to begin writing their poetry.

### Task 3, Part 1

Wulfstan first describes how he uses poetry to entertain and instruct his listeners during long evenings in the Great Hall. He offers to show the children part of one of his favourite

Figure 5.12: 'Viking Adventure' Written by Helen, Cathy and Katy of Bloodstone Group.

---

We are Cat Claw the Time-Keeper, Canute the Cook and Athelstan the Axemaker and we are fleeing from our native village because we have heard rumours that an enemy tribe of Vikings are coming our way. My two friends and I decide to take with us a cow for milk, a water cask, food and plenty of weapons. We also took a donkey to carry most of the load.

Day 1

We set off with all the load and tummies bulging with food, to the East, walking all morning and stopping to eat some berries and bread. Athelstan was milking the cow when we saw a tumbling stream. We quickly filled our water cask, finished eating our food and carried on following the stream. Suddenly we came across a wood, well a sleepy wood. Not a noise, not a stir. Then Cat Claw noticed some footprints leading away. We didn't know what it was. Then suddenly there was a noise, a deep rumble and out of the undergrowth came a wild boar. We ran and ran pushing and shoving the donkey and the cow until we had lost the wild boar. We sat down tired and exhausted and fell asleep for the night.

Day 2

We woke up in the morning and had a very light breakfast of bread, cheese and a sip of water. Then we all set off for the day with our belongings all packed up. Cat Claw suggested that we carried on following the path and we both thought that was as good an idea as any. By the time we had walked for the best bit of the morning we were all feeling tired. So we sat down and had a bite of cheese. The next bit of the journey was hard work and very tiring but it finally came to an end. By lunchtime we were at the bottom of a very desolate looking hill. We had lunch and then lost no time in ascending the hill. It was gradually beginning to get dark by the time we reached the top. There was a great view from the top and we stood there gazing at it. Suddenly, we heard a deep rumble and there behind us we saw a granite tower standing tall and proud. After the rumble came a crashing noise and the tall, proud tower collapsed. We realised that if we didn't move out of the way very quickly we would all be killed so we ran as fast as we could manage down the hill and just escaped by the skin of our teeth. After that none of us felt like walking any more so we decided to settle down for the night in the shade of a clump of trees.

Day 3

We woke up the next morning. We had a long journey from the desolate hill. We didn't really know where we were heading. We walked all morning. By dinner time we had reached a tumbling stream. There were a lot of rocks in the stream. The water looked clean so we filled our now empty water cask right to the brim. For dinner we had a small helping of vegetables and milk. It was getting dark when I heard a ghostly cry. Me and the others jumped from around the fire grabbing all our possessions with us. We ran up the stream, the sound was coming from a moored boat. Then the boat sank and a dragon ship started to appear. By the time we knew what was happening enemy Vikings were coming. We ran and ran. We came to a rope bridge. We crossed quickly, Canute drew out his cooking knife and cut the bridge down. We had to leave the cow and donkey behind. We walked for an hour, then in the distance we saw our tribe waiting for us. That night we ate a good meal before we set up camp.

---

poems and asks them if they would like a happy or a sad part. (It has to be admitted that finding a happy part in such a grim tale is not the easiest of tasks.) The children are then, according to their choice, shown short sections taken from the epic Anglo-Saxon poem Beowulf.

Wulfstan now asks the children to look at four pictures which are enclosed with the pack. Two of the pictures portray happy occasions, a coronation and a Christmas celebration taken from Anglo-Saxon life, while the other pictures depict sadder occasions, an imprisoned man and a warrior saying farewell to his family. The children are asked to choose the picture they like the most and to write down ten words which come to mind when they look at their picture. When they have done this they are asked to return to Wulfstan with their word list.

In Use. The groups adopted their usual method of working, each member first looking individually at the picture and writing his own list of ten words. This done, the groups re-formed to discuss the lists and to agree on the best ten words to be put in their group books. Figure 5.13 shows Diamond group's separate lists together with the final list agreed by the group.

Task 3, Part 2

Each group returns to the computer and is asked by Wulfstan to type in its list of ten words inspired by one of the picture cards. Wulfstan attempts to 'write' a poem by printing them on the screen in different patterns. Afterwards he informs the children that there are not yet enough words to make a good poem and suggests to them that they should attempt to

Figure 5.13: Diamond Group's Word Lists.

| Clare | Miriam | Nicola | Combined |
|---|---|---|---|
| gloomy | gloomy | gloomy | gloomy |
| misery | cold | dark | cold |
| illness | miserable | terror | lonely |
| hunger | lonely | mystery | boredom |
| boring | boredom | confusion | mystery |
| upset | dark | rotten | dingy |
| helpless | unhappy | cold | helpless |
| poor | frightened | damp | confusion |
| dingy | rotten | unhappiness | unhappy |
| dismal | hungry | lonely | dismal |

write poems of their own using the ten words along with any others they feel they need.

In Use. Once again each member of the group was asked to work independently and to try to write a poem using the ten words. When each child had had sufficient time for this the group reconvened to read each other's poems, to comment on them and to make suggestions. The children were also asked to try, if possible, to combine the separate poems into one group poem. These group poems were written in the group books and illustrated by a picture which conveyed the mood of the poem. The separate poems of the individuals of Diamond group are shown in Figure 5.14 together with their group poem.

An examination of these poems reveals how the children's images were refined and simplified during the discussions to produce a workmanlike, though perhaps rather uninspired, combined poem. Compare this to the poem shown in Figure 5.15 which was written by one individual who was inspired by the picture of a soldier leaving his family to go to war.

## COMPLETING WULFSTAN'S WORDHOARD

When they have written their poem each group of children returns to the computer. Wulfstan welcomes them in familiar fashion and congratulates them on completing the three tasks of Wordhoard. They are no longer apprentices but Wordsmiths and a certificate celebrating their achievement is duly displayed on the screen.

Figure 5.14: Diamond Group's Set of Poems.

---

Nicola's Poem

In a dark gloomy cell,
It was very dismal.
The man was in confusion,
In the cold.
He was unhappy and lonely.
The mystery came to boredom
In the dingy cell.

Clare's Poem

In a gloomy cold lonely cell,
A man lay there in his boredom and confusion.
It was a dingy dismal dungeon.
Thinking about his family,
Helpless, unhappiness,
In the mystery in the dark.

Miriam's Poem

The gloomy cold and dingy cell,
A man lying in mystery and confusion.
Helpless and unhappy,
Changes to boredom
In the dismal prison cell

The Combined Poem

In a gloomy cold cell
A man lay there lonely and unhappy,
Wishing for his family.
The cell was dingy and dismal,
Thinking of the boredom of his future life,
His helpless confusion remained a mystery.

---

## ASSESSING THE PROJECT

The above descriptions of the program WULFSTAN'S WORDHOARD and of the project stemming from it would be incomplete without some discussion of the methods of working which were adopted and without some evaluation of what had been achieved.

The primary importance of a project such as this is that most of the work done by the children is, in fact, carried out away from the computer and is undertaken in a collaborative way.

Figure 5.15: A Poem Written as Part of Task 3, WORDHOARD.

Departure by Christian

As they said their farewells
Tears flowed like a tumbling stream.
They were sorrowful, but
Knew it must be done.

Determination flowed through his veins,
But horror crept in.
Though he looked fearless,
Inside he was like a squirrel.

Horror rose up before his eyes
And stared him right in the face,
An arrow pierced his eye
And bravely he fell dead.

Bad news travelled fast
And his wife was broken-hearted.
She shared the sadness with her friends
And together they mourned.

Primary school teachers need no convincing that purposeful discussion is important to children's language development but often have difficulty in finding a context in which the discussion might take place without it being dominated by one vociferous and over-influential individual. Working in small groups not only demands contributions from each member but, with the right resources, can also provide positive support to each member of the group.

The method of working described above, in which each child initially undertakes the task alone, means that all members of the group will have had the opportunity to think about the task before discussion actually takes place. All members should, then, be familiar with the activity which helps to prevent some of the more depressing outcomes of group discussion such as excessive divergence, or dominance by a single individual or, perhaps, worst of all complete lack of any idea of what the group is supposed to be doing. It is also important that children should have had the chance to think things through on their own so that they can make personal contributions whilst at the same time learning from each other.

The person of Wulfstan provides a reference point for criticising how effective the children's writing is and for judging what it is they are supposed to be doing. This makes a very worthwhile change from the more usual situation where the class teacher is the sole arbiter. To expect young children to be self-critical is a tall order unless we provide them with a user-friendly model or a half-way house. However considerate teachers may try to be, their critical influence children's creative work can be a negative experience not only in dramatic activities but also in the tricky business of getting children to rewrite what they have already enjoyed doing.

Some teachers may have seen the Schools Council film, 'Take Three', made by the Learning Through Drama Project in which a teacher, Don Hendy, takes a class of eleven-year-olds through a drama lesson. The children were asked to work in small groups and to invent an 'essence machine' in which their own movements and voices created the effects. Predictably, 'Essence of a Haunted House' was the popular choice and could have led to complete disorder and dissatisfaction on the part of both children and teacher. But, in order to help the children generate their own self-critical control over detail, Don Hendy invented a critic who could see everything but who existed at the end of a telephone line. By pretending to hold a telephone conversation with the critic the teacher was able to pass on ideas and suggestions without too much personal involvement. Wulfstan performs a similar role in the project described above.

## SOME REFLECTIONS

The working methods described above are very much in accordance with the view that children learn better by doing rather than by being told. A skill is acquired more easily when it is needed to perform a task than when it is being learned as an exercise or as a practice run for some future use. The children taking part in the project were constantly acquiring new skills while using them for specific purposes. They were involved in quite searching discussions; their writing showed considerable thought in a variety of forms (descriptive, narrative and poetic); they made books, paper sculptures, maps and model villages; they criticised, argued and made group decisions about procedures and developments.

The computer, throughout the project, played an active though subservient role. The imaginary guide and taskmaster, Wulfstan, initiated and suggested activities but, as time went on, became less important to the project as the activities and their products increased in their own right. It is an interesting statistic that, although the project described above lasted six weeks, the time spent at the computer for any one child totalled less than 50 minutes.

WULFSTAN'S WORDHOARD provides an excellent platform for mounting a primary language project in which children are moving constantly between the assimilation of new vocabulary and new ideas and the exploration and re-working of their own knowledge and experience.

NOTES

1. Robert C. Akers, Single Section Bookbinding (Dryad Leaflet No. 530, 1980).

Chapter Six

# PROGRAMS FOR INVESTIGATING LANGUAGE

In primary schools today it would be rare indeed to find a separate block in the school timetable allocated to the subject 'English' yet the reverse is true in secondary schools where English constitutes a major feature of the timetable. English has the special administrative advantage of infinite flexibility in that it can take place anywhere at anytime being realisable in such relatively simple terms as 30 or so bottoms sitting at suitable desk tops on 30 or so chairs.

So far as the curriculum and public examinations are concerned, of which the timetable is an outward and visible sign, the status of English as a school subject is very strong indeed yet most secondary teachers, are aware of questions now being raised in different quarters about the legitimacy of English as a separate subject area. Some of these questions stem from a philosophical approach to curriculum content which is itself part of a wider educational reappraisal of the subject-centred curriculum. Others are more political in origin and reflect socio-economic changes which affect secondary schools in obviously direct ways e.g. unemployment and technological change.

The Connecticut Study (see Chapter One) reflects this climate of doubt and potential change in asking teachers if they thought that English would eventually disappear as a school subject to be replaced by a task force of 'linguistic trouble-shooters'. Many teachers of English have in recent years shifted toward the view that English is not so much a body of knowledge as the space between the bodies of knowledge and have formulated their syllabuses in terms of the four language modes - reading, writing, talking and listening. This is not the same thing as becoming a service industry for the rest of the curriculum but moves closer to aims and principles more clearly recognisable in primary schools. There is, however, a further question at issue which is common to both primary and secondary schools and that is the distinction often made between 'skills' and 'experience' in language learning and English teaching.

We have made these preliminary remarks and raised the last question because there seems to be a central problem in all teaching schemes designed to develop language skills or to improve language knowledge and that is the danger of reducing the living language to a mechanical activity of de-contextualised routines or a set of abstractions; something which, in everyday use, it demonstrably is not. Many teachers, in both the primary and secondary sectors, are concerned that current demands for the teaching of language skills and sub-skills and for the setting of precise, measurable, age-related objectives in language development, will generate a negative emphasis on what children cannot do rather than a positive emphasis on what they can do. Many argue that skills can only have meaning when set in an appropriate environment of first-hand experience with opportunities for exploration. Such an environment is of course difficult to create and sustain given the constraints placed upon individual teachers, whereas it is much easier to identify a set of skills and objectives and devise a syllabus of work toward those ends.

Reading schemes are easy to construct but they do not necessarily help children to make meanings out of what they read. Much evidence suggests that children learn to read in spite of, rather than because of, the school's chosen reading scheme. Teaching children to read for meaning, to comprehend and learn from what they have read is a far more difficult, long-term proposition. Similarly it has proved quite easy to design drill and practice programs but extremely time consuming to imagine and produce good content-free or open programs.

This chapter is concerned with programs which focus on some aspect of linguistic knowledge or skill in the light of the following principles:

- That a skills approach to teaching the language arts is perfectly reasonable provided it is recognised that language skills are peculiarly cognitive skills i.e. there are things that we need to KNOW (whether explicitly or intuitively) in order to perform the appropriate skills.
- Some form of language awareness usually precedes knowledge about language.
- That explicit knowledge about language is often arrived at through discussion with others and through the experience of other people's responses to our own language use.

Consider, as an introduction, the following example of language investigation in which the computer played no part.

## TRANSLATING ANGLO-SAXON

This work was undertaken by a group of eleven-year-old children.

The class were presented with a copy of the Lord's Prayer written in 10th Century English and produced in a facsimile of Anglo-Saxon script. The children were not informed as to the content of the writing but were told that it was 'a sort of poem' which would be familiar to them if they could translate the 'old-fashioned' language. The prayer is reproduced in Figure 6.1.

Initial discussions centred on the methods by which the contents of a language could change and what the main influences of change could be. It was also suggested to the children that, although language could change almost beyond recognition in the space of 1000 years, it might still be possible to recognise some items of its vocabulary as being similar to words still in present-day use.

The children were asked to make a copy of the 'poem' in script as closely resembling the original as possible. At the same time they were asked to look carefully at the words - something difficult not to do when copying material which appears to the reader to have no meaning - and to try to think of modern words which resembled, in some way, the words in the poem. An inspection of the piece in Figure 6.1 shows that a proportion of the words contained in it can be seen to have similarities to present-day words - an obvious example being the phrase 'forgyf us ure gyltas'.

After a short while two of the children, out of earshot of the remainder of the class, tentatively suggested that the piece might be the Lord's Prayer and, as time went on, more and more children came to the same conclusion. Other suggestions were also made, e.g. 'something from the bible' and, when most of the class had successfully solved this lingustic puzzle, the remainder had their attention drawn to the phrase mentioned above - 'forgyf us ure gyltas' - as a clue.

As the children completed their copies of the prayer they began to make impromptu attempts at translating parts of it and it was suggested to them that this would be made easier if the modern version of the prayer were written at the side to facilitate easy comparison. It was also suggested that, when the modern counterpart of a word was identified, it should be written over the top of the original thus eliminating, one by one, the words which they couldn't understand.

In due course this translation process was continued as a class activity enabling the children to make their suggestions for the translation of different words and to give the reasons for their choices. The meanings of the remaining words were sometimes guessed at and, occasionally, this brought out unexpected and pleasing items of interest. For

Figure 6.1: Lord's Prayer in Tenth Century English, by Ellis.

Faeder ure þuþe eart on heo-
fonum si þin nama gehalgod. To
þecume þin rice. Geweorþe ðin
willa on eorðan swa swa on he-
ofonum. Urne daeghwamlican
hlaf syle us to daeg. And forgyf us ure gytas, swa swa we
forgfaþ urum gyltendum. and
ne galaed þu us on costnunge,
ae alys us of yfele.

Suplice

instance, it became clear from an examination of the surrounding words, that the repeated words 'swa swa' should be translated, 'as'. This initially puzzled children and teacher who were surprised and then pleased to notice that the middle two letters of 'swa swa' do, in fact, spell 'as'!

Few people would argue that this activity was not of interest and benefit to the children, yet the variety of skills brought into play at any given point are extremely interwoven. Surprisingly, perhaps, concentration on something written over 1000 years ago led the children into an investigation of modern English usage.

Consider the methods used by the children in translating this particular piece. Recognising the work as the Lord's Prayer is something of an achievement requiring the careful comparison of many unfamiliar words to the contents of one's own vocabulary. This can only be done by drawing on an intuitive understanding of language in order to formulate the rules needed to solve a succession of problems. It also requires the translator to allow his mind to 'free-wheel' whilst inspecting the piece so that diverse and subtle connections may be explored. As an illustration of the quality of the language experience afforded by this kind of work contrast it with a conventional exercise requiring children merely to change the tenses of verbs contained in, say, ten sentences.

The computer is an ideal aid for this kind of investigative work especially when there is an element of problem-solving involved. Two problem solving activities which have proved especially fruitful in investigative approaches to, for example, reading difficult texts, are sequencing and word deletion. These are now very familiar as pen and paper approaches but the word deletion computer program par excellence is Bob Moy's DEVELOPING TRAY.

## DEVELOPING TRAY

DEVELOPING TRAY, published by MEP, is a program which presents a total cloze passage in which no words or letters are shown, merely the punctuation. What the user first sees on the screen is a galaxy of commas and full stops looking rather like an opening sequence for Patrick Moore's 'Sky at Night'. The user is given an initial score which can then be bartered in order to 'buy' letters and which increases upon the successful prediction of any letters in the passage. The letters added to the passage appear in a seemingly random pattern and resemble the way parts of a photograph come into focus before others as it is immersed in a photographer's developing tray - from which the program takes its name.

DEVELOPING TRAY provides an option of using a 'scratchpad' which is a blank screen provided for the user to work out ideas before entering his predictions into the passage. Whenever the scratchpad is used it adds 50 to the user's score. Many teachers agree that, whilst it is desirable to be able to experiment with the scratchpad in this way, they frequently resort to one of the oldest word-processors known to man, namely pencil and paper! Doing so, however, means the loss of the opportunity to increase the score by using a scratchpad but, as the users become more and more involved in the activity, so scoring seems to become less and less important.

Although the program is supplied with three passages which are more suitable for older children and adults than primary age children it is a simple matter to tailor any passage for use with TRAY. A CREATE program is supplied which allows this to be done and the results saved as a file on disc which can then be called up by the main program. A further option allows part-completed passages to be saved at any point and restarted at a later date a feature which provides the teacher with a useful option. It is possible, for example, to prepare a text for a specific purpose e.g. to concentrate on particular word classes or on the structure of words from which parts have been deleted.

Anyone using DEVELOPING TRAY soon finds he is absorbed in the activity and is usually delighted when a particularly tricky piece of decoding is solved. The reasons for this are not difficult to find since, in its extreme form, the problem presented seems virtually impossible to solve yet, by the gradual discovery and application of rules which govern the use of language, users are amazed to find that the solution is not impossible after all.

Most teachers would agree that the program works to its full advantage, as is so often the case, when operated by two or three children. It focusses their attention and conversation on apparently small but important aspects of language. To be faced with a blank screen and to be told that the words of a passage are hidden there waiting to be discovered is exciting in prospect but can also be daunting. In order to make a start the children need to develop an initial strategy with which to attack the problem. There are a number of successful ways of doing this but most of them involve recognising that some letters and some words occur more frequently in our language than others. 'Buying' some of these letters gives children something to work with. This process is illustrated in Figure 6.2 which is an excerpt from a dialogue during a session of TRAY.

Once some letters have been inserted in the passage the results must be closely examined. The children must, as suggested earlier, use their intuitive knowledge of how words are constructed and of the conventions which govern their use, in order to make informed predictions about the contents of the passage. This can be seen in the Figure 6.3 which is an excerpt from a session of TRAY in which two eleven-year-

Figure 6.2: A Transcript of Children's Conversation During a Session with TRAY.

---

| | |
|---|---|
| Cathy: | Predict 'e'. There's always a lot of e's. |
| Karen: | OK... Yes, hundreds. |
| Cathy: | That must be the title up there. |
| Karen: | That could be 'here' |
| Cathy: | Try an 'h'. |
| Karen: | What, predict it? |
| Cathy: | Yes. |
| Karen: | Predict 'h' and 'r'. Oh, it's right. |
| Cathy: | Yeah... You get 6 for a right answer. |
| Karen: | Oh, good. |
| Karen: | That's the end of a word, that must be the end of a word. |
| Cathy: | Shall we buy a letter? Buy the letter 't'? |
| Karen: | OK. We'll buy the letter 't'; return. |
| Cathy: | T is a good one; 't' and 'a'. |
| Karen: | 't' and 'a'; what about 't-a'? It might help us a bit. |
| Cathy: | We're not buying any of them, just 't' |
| Karen: | 't is already in the text so buying costs nothing'. |
| Both: | Oh, yeah. |
| Cathy: | Look for the 'theres'. |
| Karen: | Hmm. That'll be one there, won't it? |
| Cathy: | Predict 'h'. Yes! |
| Karen: | Yes!...There's another one there. |
| Cathy: | We're very good at this. |
| Karen: | Oh, yeah. |
| Cathy: | That might be one there, if that's an 'e'. |
| Karen: | Yes... No, the 'e' would have come up wouldn't it? |

---

Figure 6.3: A Transcript of Children's Conversation During a Session of TRAY.

---

| | |
|---|---|
| Jim: | What can that be - blank, u, i, e, t, something? |
| Chris: | Yes, it's funny, that 'u'. |
| Jim: | How many letters in front of the 'u'? |
| Chris: | Don't know; maybe two? |
| Jim: | That might be 'very'? |
| Chris: | 'Very something'...something u, i...' |
| Jim: | 'Quiet'? It might be 'quiet'. |
| Chris: | Hmm. It fits. Try it, predict it. |
| Jim: | Predict, q. Yes. It's quiet. |
| Chris: | If it's 'very' it must be 'quietly'. |

---

olds were constructing a passage taken from Roald Dahl's 'Charlie and the Chocolate Factory'.

DEVELOPING TRAY depends upon fairly large chunks of language e.g. whole paragraphs in order that children should have some contextual guidance for their successive guesses. It seems to alternate between guessing and logical thinking with guessing becoming progressively less necessary as the syntax and cohesion of the passage emerge. Other programs look more closely at individual sentences and individual words. The children make little contribution from their own 'wordhoards' on the screen itself but the program stimulate a lot of investigative and collaborative talk.

SWITCHIT, for example, focusses children's minds on specific aspects of language use but does not limit their capacity for creative uses of language.

## SWITCHIT

SWITCHIT, published by MEP, was originally designed as part of an MEP Project. It is a story-writing program in which children are required to provide a series of lexical alternatives.

It is very easy to forget that any published material has been carefully scrutinised for misspellings or incorrect punctuation and has been redrafted over a period of time. Teachers, however, often seem to expect children to write 200 or so words correctly structured, spelt and punctuated in one draft and within the space of an hour! Convinced of the importance of their writing and so often willing to try, children nevertheless face a variety of difficulties. Without exception they respond gratefully to any help they are offered especially where the composition of their stories is concerned. The journey section of WULFSTAN'S WORDHOARD and the structures in MICROSTORY provide clear examples of this.

Once they have started their writing, children are very quickly caught up in the main business of story-telling and one would not expect them to give much attention to spelling and punctuation, editorial skills best left until later when the flow has ebbed. The time and place for editorial skills, however, has to be nicely judged by the teacher. The chief danger of leaving them until the end is that they can easily be forgotten. Researchers on the National Writing Project, however, confirm that children never forget their shortcomings and despair over cumulative neglect every bit as much as their teachers. But between sustaining the narrative flow and tidying up the spelling and punctuation there is another element of writing - namely the choosing of alternative words. The ability to search around for the right word is relevant to the flow but is often relegated to the editorial skills. 'Right' here does not necessarily mean a 'better' word which the teacher has thought of, but the child's own recognition that an alternative word is more suited to what he wants to say. Sometimes the discovery of an alternative word can change the way a character is being written about and even change the direction of the narrative.

SWITCHIT provides a structure for story-writing and, at the same time, encourages the children to concentrate on using the most fitting word from their vocabularies. It does so by introducing a story and asking the children to change its context. Thus, if the story was about a horse race, for example, the children might be require to alter it to a story about a Grand Prix car race. Any reference to the 'operator' of the horse as a rider would then require changing to, say, 'driver' as a more fitting word. This simple idea is the kernel of the SWITCHIT suite of programs.

The suite contains three programs all of which display four pictures - one 'core' picture and three others from which the user chooses the one which interests him most. A short story is displayed featuring the subject of the core picture; the user is required to alter this story so that it features the subject of the picture he has chosen. This story, which may be a similar one to the original or a totally different one, can be printed out on completion or saved as a file on disc. The form of this file is such that it can be recovered not only by the program itself but by the word processing program WORDWISE thus providing the writer with the option of developing the story further.

Each of the three programs contained in the suite SWITCHIT has a different theme associated with it as follows:

- SWITCHIT1 has the theme 'speed'. The subject of the core picture and story is a racehorse; the other pictures are of a racing bicycle, a racing motorcycle and a Grand Prix racing car.
- SWITCHIT2 has the theme 'survival'. The subject of the core picture and the story is an Arab riding a camel; the other pictures are of a lunar astronaut, a scuba diver and an Eskimo.
- SWITCHIT3 has the theme 'predators'. The subject of the core picture and the story is a fox; the other pictures are of a ladybird, a kestrel and a pike.

It will be appreciated that the pictures in the program play an important role - that of providing inspiration and information for a story - and thus should bear comparison with those printed in books. With this in mind they have been prepared using a graphics tablet and contain a wealth of fine detail not normally found in computer-displayed pictures. An example is given in Figure 6.4.

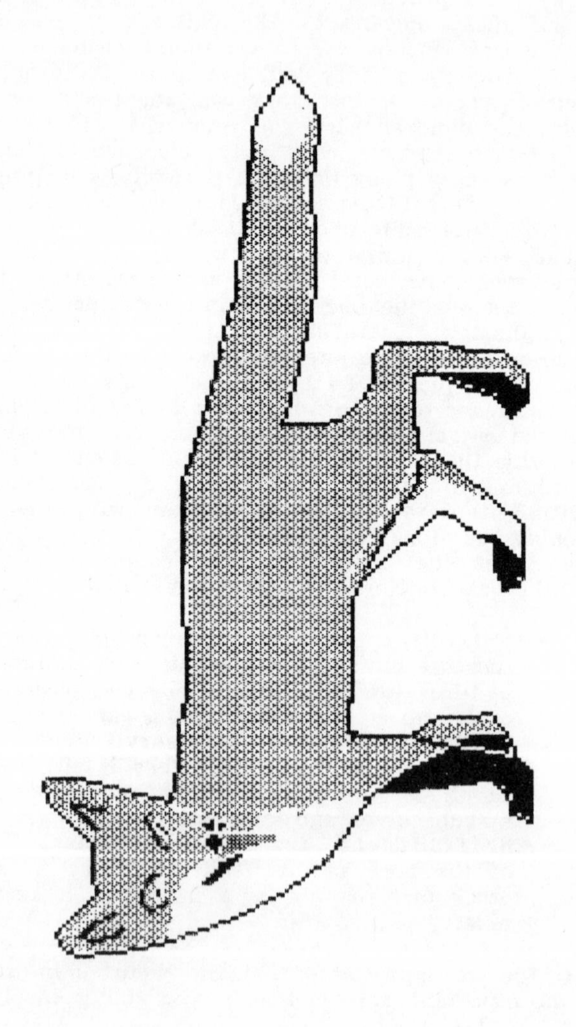

Figure 6.4: Fox Picture from SWITCHIT4.

In operation, SWITCHIT1, for instance, first shows the pictures and asks the user to choose the one he regards the most interesting. The core picture, that of the racehorse, is shown and also a six-sentence story featuring the racehorse. This story is reproduced in Figure 6.5.

Figure 6.5: Core Story from SWITCHIT1.

---

```
Silver, the Arab grey stallion / galloped strongly / across
the racecourse turf.
Approaching the final jump / the jockey tightened the rein /
and nudged his heels against the horse's flanks.
The magnificent animal responded / and effortlessly cleared
the barrier / with a loud snort.
Glancing over his shoulder, the jockey / could see the other
steeds behind him / and realised that he could win if Silver's
breath held.
Suddenly the stallion stumbled / and the rider struggled to
keep his seat / as Silver regained his balance.
Loud applause broke out as they passed the winning post / and
Silver slowed to a proud trot.
```

---

The user is asked to alter the subject of this story to that of the picture previously chosen. The core story is then displayed and, as each sentence is shown, one phrase at a time is displayed in a different colour from the others indicating that it is the one currently being changed. The user types in a new phrase which takes the place of the original phrase. The next phrase or sentence is then considered. The oblique lines in Figure 6.5 indicate these phrases.

At any time during the proceedings users may opt to see the entire original story or their own story so far written or their subject picture. They may also save a partly written story for later completion.

The program encourages children to write a story based, however loosely, upon the core story. Since the subject of the story has been changed - for instance, from racehorse to, say, racing cycle in SWITCHIT 1 - this means that the context has also altered and that any words specific to that context must also be changed. Thus, in our example, any reference to the jockey, i.e. the 'operator' of the horse, must be replaced with a word which applies specifically to the 'operator' of a racing cycle. Finding 'the right word' and becoming aware of appropriate sets of related words is an important part of writing and one in which novice writers are thrown very much upon their own resources. Recognising that one change can set in motion a whole series of choices and changes is a revelation for many and proves a stimulus not only to use dictionaries and reference books but also to create a personal thesaurus of words and phrases.

The program uses the child's phrases to replace those in the original story whilst retaining any not altered. If, for instance, we continue with our example and replace "Silver, the Arab Grey stallion" with the phrase "The blue Peugeot racing cycle" the program will display this sentence:

> The blue Peugeot racing cycle / galloped strongly / across the racecourse turf.

It is now apparent that the phrase "galloped strongly" is unsuitable in the new context and must be altered, perhaps to "sped smoothly". The program will now display the following:

> The blue Peugeot racing cycle / sped smoothly / across the racecourse turf.

In this way words which are out of context are made obvious and can be replaced. This is best done by children working together so that they can discuss possibilities and share ideas.

An example of the program in action is given by Figures 6.6 and 6.7 which reproduce the original story of SWITCHIT2 - SURVIVAL together with a story written by two eleven-year-olds.

Figures 6.8 and 6.9 show a further example of the original story from SWITCHIT3 - PREDATORS - together with a story written by two girls of eleven.

Figure 6.6: The Core Story from SWITCHIT2 - SURVIVAL.

---

```
Ahkbed, a deeply tanned Arab / firmly reined in his faithful
camel / in the midst of the arid desert.
Overhead a fierce sun beat down / baking the landscape of
endless sand, / the horizon shimmering in the heat.
Ahkbed dismounted / and gazed at the sparse vegetation and
featureless sandhills / in this desolate part of the world.
He thought of the oasis / a mere ten kilometres ride away /
and of the cool water and shade he would enjoy there.
Suddenly his attention was caught by an object / lying
half-buried in the hot sand.
As he knelt in the sunlight / he inspected his precious find /
and smiled contentedly to himself.
```

---

Figure 6.7: A Story Written by Chris and James Using SWITCHIT2 - SURVIVAL.

---

Neil Armstrong,an extremely brave American / firmly gripped his trusty camera / in the midst of the Sea of Tranquillity.
Overhead in the vast emptiness of space / he saw a massive meteorite streaking across the solar system / heading for Mars.
Neil Armstrong threw a rock and watched it disappear / and he went into his lunar spacecraft. / He floated about a bit eating dehydrated cabbage.
He thought of his relatives / and their worries for him. / He then went to join Buzz in the spacecraft.
Suddenly his attention was caught by an object / lying half-buried in the dust.
As he cleared the dust off it / Neil realised it was a piece of Vostok 1 / Yuri Gagarin's space ship.

---

In our earlier description of SWITCHIT it was mentioned that the children's story can be saved on disc in such a form that the WORDWISE word processor program can retrieve it. This is a very useful feature for encouraging children to redraft and refine their work. In earlier discussions it was mentioned that the problem with asking children to redraft their writing was that they often produced insufficient material for this to be meaningful. Using a program like SWITCHIT enables children to construct a story which can be expanded, reshaped and redrafted at will using a word

Figure 6.8: The Core Story from SWITCHIT3 - PREDATORS.

---

The fox is a large mammal / and is well equipped to hunt its prey of rabbits and small rodents.
His body is covered in red fur / and his four sturdy legs / enable him to run at a very fast rate.
When foxes are first born they are called cubs / and spend their first weeks in the fox's earth, / looked after by their mother the vixen.
Soon they leave the earth and learn to hunt insects, / copying the behavior of their parents.
When they are old enough they leave their family / to hunt for themselves and eventually find a mate and have a family of cubs of their own.
Although foxes do some damage / the woods of England would be poorer places without their presence.

---

Figure 6.9: A Story Written by Cathy and Kerry Using SWITCHIT3 - PREDATORS.

---

The pike is mainly a river fish / and can protect and defend itself whenever needed.
Its prey includes smaller fish and other pike.
A pikes body is covered with silvery scales / and its six fins enable it to swim at a very fast rate.
When the fry are first born they are very small / and spend their first few days in a particular part of the river, / looking after themselves.
Soon they leave their home.They hunt their prey / and eventually find a mate and have a family of their own.
They are a much liked fish / and in France they are a great delicacy.

---

processor. It is possible that programs such as SWITCHIT and MICROSTORY will find favour in the classroom because they provide not only starting points but outlines of work which can give real significance to the use of a word processor.

## OTHER PROGRAMS FOR INVESTIGATING LANGUAGE

### PODD

PODD is published by ASK. It is a deceptively simple program focussing on the use of verbs.

PODD is a cartoon character who appears on the screen with the words, 'Podd can ...'. The user types in a verb to complete the sentence and, if it is one of the 100 or so which the program recognises, Podd will perform it. If something is typed in which the program does not have on its list the program responds with, 'No, he can't'. Examples of things Podd can do are 'fly' (in which he sprouts wings and flies about the screen) and 'hop' (in which arms and legs appear allowing him to hop about the screen).

The program provides an ideal activity for infants and lower juniors to explore the use of verbs and begin to recognise how they may be classed as action words. Having a computer set up in a corner running PODD would enable children to think up action words, discuss them with other children and try them out on the computer. If their idea is a successful one it could be added to a list which would lengthen over a period of time as the children became more searching.

If you tire of PODD you can always tell him to vanish. He does!

WELLIES

WELLIES, developed by MEP and acquired by Prestel, is a program designed to allow children to explore conjunctions.

The program displays two phrases 'it is raining' (or 'it rains') and 'I wear my wellington boots' (or 'I am wearing my wellington boots') which are joined by various conjunctions, for example, 'because', 'even if' and 'in case'. The children are asked to decide whether or not the sentence makes sense and, if not, are asked to try to rearrange the sentence so that it does make sense.

WELLIES has the appearance of a drill and practice program except for one major difference; it stimulates curiosity rather than routine performance. It is not designed to teach a series of correct responses but to encourage discussion about what makes sense and what is nonsense in English sentences.

By focussing on words which connect statements it alerts pupils to some logical and stylistic features of English syntax. By stimulating talk it also makes them aware of the ways in which intonation can carry or alter the literal meaning of a sentence. The program was derived from a table top game consisting of small cards, some of which contained statements while others contained conjunctions e.g. 'although', 'if', 'whenever', 'since', 'despite', 'because'. The computer version is not only easier to manage but offers a much more concentrated experience to which children respond with enthusiasm. It would be an easy program for teachers to misuse if it were not for the fact that it is self contained and that two or three children will work at it voluntarily with a mixture of curiosity and amused irritation. Frequently they leave the computer arguing furiously about whether a sentence can or can not be made to make sense. Figure 6.10 is a brief example from three ten-year-olds.

Figure 6.10: A Transcript of Children's Conversation Whilst Using WELLIES.

---

Paul: 'If I wear my wellington boots it rains.' Does that make sense?
Kevin: Yes.
Jane: No.
Paul: 'If it rains I wear my wellington boots.' That makes sense.
Kevin: Yes.
Jane: Yes. 'It rains if I wear my wellington boots.' That doesn't make sense.
Paul: They'd have to be magic wellies.
Kevin: How do you mean?

---

There followed a long explanation from Jane and Paul of how the wellies would have to be magic in order to make it rain. At one point they imagined somebody doing a rain dance wearing wellington boots which eventually brought a grin of understanding to Kevin's face. At other times children have been observed to produce the most ingenious intonation patterns in order to make some sense of a sentence displayed on the screen. They are also prepared to argue very thoughtfully if they disagree with either the computer or their partners.

Wellies is, in effect, a language game rather than a teaching program but a game in which children reflect upon some of the ways in which simple sentences may be joined into complex ones. There is no suggestion that long sentences are necessarily better than short ones; the emphasis throughout is on the meaning and use of the connecting words and on differences which can be made by changing the order of the two statements in each sentence.

## WORDWEB

WORDWEB is published by ESM and is a picture thesaurus. Although originally designed for use by deaf children the program has enormous potential in any infant school.

WORDWEB comes on five discs, one being a management disc which controls the use of four others devoted to different topics: the street, the farm, the home and the zoo. Up to 100 pictures can be accessed within each topic and are manipulated by the accompanying text. Each key word has a number of illustrations associated with it so that children can explore their commonality by viewing the different pictures. Children choose their own pathways through the program and, with the printer option engaged, this pathway can be studied at a later date by the teacher. Janet Holdsworth, the instigator of the program, has found, for example, that children repeatedly view the same few pages until they understand the meaning of the same word in different contexts.

Designers of language programs usually have to achieve a compromise between constraint and continuity in language use. The structure required in order to present the program user with something to think about must not be so rigid that it severely limits HOW the user will think through the problem or task presented. WORDWEB allows users to wander along paths and to make linguistic connections which they choose for themselves at any given point in the program. Thus the computer is made to follow the user's thought patterns and within the context of whichever accompanying picture is on the screen, it will print sentences generated by the users. In its present published form specific attention is paid to the use of verbs but there seems no reason why the principle cannot be extended to the use of prepositions and adverbs.

## SOME REFLECTIONS

In the 1960s claims were made in primary and secondary schools for the rejection of grammar and explicit 'language teaching' in favour of original writing, drama and the development of oracy. It looked like an ideological shift from the arid abstractions of grammar which had proved singularly un-transferable as learning experiences, to a new creativity which promised better opportunities for personal growth and the development of language skills. In fact what had really happened was that the new spirit in English teaching offered an excuse for the systematic neglect of grammar on the grounds that the tradition of grammar teaching derived from the classical prejudices of grammarians such as Bishop Lowth whose 'Short Introduction to English Grammar' was published in 1762. The essentially prescriptive tradition ignored the native competence of English speakers, censured the supposed deficiencies of their written style and advocated rules which took no account of the differences between speech and writing and what were, in any case, of dubious origin and validity.

It has now become apparent that we have neglected grammar to our cost and in the process made it difficult for newer, descriptive grammars and investigative approaches to language to gain general acceptance. Descriptive grammars are quite different from prescriptive ones and relate much more closely and usefully to the mental processes which lie behind the planning of speech and writing. To become aware of this difference teachers need to keep in mind the fundamental things with which grammar is concerned - e.g. defining time and number (conjugations); locating persons, places and things in space (pronouns and prepositions); identifying the main focus of attention (the subject); making connections (conjunctions); the sequencing and organisation of ideas and information (word order and syntax) - rather than worry about dubious stylistic recommendations for formal writing e.g. never end sentence with a preposition; never begin them with conjunctions; every sentence must contain at least one finite verb.

At the beginning of this chapter, as elsewhere, we implied that there are plenty of ways to teach English badly, yet few ways to do it well since so much depends upon the teacher's own perceptions and linguistic awareness. Language arts software will not solve problems of grammar overnight any more than word processors will solve age old problems of writing. What it can do is focus the concentrated attention children are willing to give to computers, and direct it into thoughtful investigations of how the English language works in everyday use. Used in this spirit good software has the potential to rescue the grammar recommendations made in the DES pamphlet 'English: From 5 to 16' (HMSO, 1984) from traditional errors and turn them into creative learning.

There has been a traditional scepticism about the value of explicit knowledge about language yet it is no less interesting than other kinds of knowledge and at least as 'useful' for human understanding as History, Biology, Geology or Physics. The new JMB A level English Language syllabus, admittedly somewhat distant from the primary years, nevertheless nails its colours firmly to the mast in arresting the aim that students 'should be able to use language better by knowing more about it'. With WORDWEB children can begin a journey toward that A level via an increasing range of software (e.g. PODD, SWITCHIT, WELLIES, DEVELOPING TRAY and the writing programs in Chapter 3) which will encourage them to reflect on their intuitive knowledge about language, to investigate varieties of and to formulate their own ideas about the nature and function of language in human communication.

Chapter Seven

# WORD PROCESSING

In a very important sense, everything we have said so far has been about word processing if, by that term, we mean children using a computer to think with and using language to put their thoughts in writing. Once teachers start to use micros seriously it is not long before they begin to examine more critically the nature of thinking and the role played by language in our thought processes. The tendency, for example, to view thinking as a unitary, intentional and entirely logical process (or to think that it SHOULD BE all these things) soon gives way to a recognition of the different shapes and sizes in which thinking actually takes place. The variety of thinking and language strategies displayed by children using deceptively simple programs offers almost a ready made syllabus for intellectual development provided the contexts are appropriately varied and significant for the children themselves.

Thinking is not often a systematic plumbing of unfathomable depths for profound and definitive statements; nor is it usually a carefully measured journey on precisely laid tracks. Frequently we hardly think at all in a purposeful, 'efficient' way but simply trace familiar short circuits, or make habitual responses. On the occasions when we do think in a conscious way we often go through a process of pushing words and ideas around in the head, sometimes playfully, sometimes guided by intuition. It is not unusual, for example, to think of two or more ideas at once or to find alternative words and phrases slipping in and out of mental focus. The mind copes with ambiguities and metaphors daily, not just in poetic literature, but in ordinary language, a phenomenon which can be very effectively exploited by advertisers. One pharmaceutical manufacturer, for example, can say of a pain reliever on television, 'You don't need a doctor's prescription', whilst at the same moment displaying on the screen the words 'Available only from your pharmacist'. This is a very clever way of blending two conflicting ideas in a single instantaneous thought; easy access plus protection, independence plus security.

But for every coherent thought, whether simple or complex, there are a thousand irrelevancies and inconsistencies wittingly or unwittingly present. Even when the mind is generating a single train of thought, other thoughts and half-formed ideas are interwoven with it. Sometimes the mind backtracks, sometimes it reformulates, often it repeats itself. Frequently it grinds to a halt. All these only too familiar behaviours, and many more, are reflected in that well known form of talk we usually refer to as 'thinking aloud'.

Given then that our thought patterns may occur in varied shapes, verbal and non-verbal, and proceed in unpredictable ways, it is not surprising that the process of writing them down can be so difficult. Writing converts thoughts and feelings into linear sequences; it is by nature a linear or syntactic process ironing out thought into consecutive, cohesive and coherent sentence patterns. The contemporary sense of urgency for communication often neglects the fact that a function of language, at least equal to that of communication is the use of language for giving meanings to one's own experiences. 'How can I tell what I think until I see what I have said?' has almost become a modern proverb.

In recent years we have begun to pay more and more attention to the thinking that goes on behind the writing while the increasing use of word processors has also thrown into prominence the structural, compositional and ideational aspects of writing.

## THE WORD PROCESSOR IN THE CLASSROOM

In industry and commerce word processors save time and money; in the classroom word processors should allow children the unaccustomed luxury of being able to play around with words. It is recognised that redrafting of text is a necessary process for anyone wishing to become a 'writer' rather than merely a 'scribe' but it is not easy to convince children of this fact when they are faced with the effort of rewriting a whole page for the improvement of one sentence. Once they have discovered the ease with which alterations in text can be made with a word processor, adult writers take delight in this new-found ability to polish their work and some report a sudden and pleasing improvement in their writing. We cannot deny children the same experience.

It is difficult to define what makes a piece of writing 'good'. The choice of words and the syntactical constructions have something to so with it. Imagination and wit may also be important. Add to these two skills such qualities as flair, imagination and wit, say, and we may be some way towards that elusive definition. If the word processor has a contribution to make then it must be in the areas of composition and style as well as in editing and formatting. One of the criticisms highlighted by the Bullock Report on the teaching of language was that teachers gave too much attention to the surface mechanical features of writing - spelling, punctuation, for example - and too little to developing composition, content and style.

Teachers have rightly celebrated the new mastery word processing has given children over the appearance of their writing. Even if it never reaches the stage of a printout, children's writing looks so much more professional on the VDU screen. Its transcription into that medium enables young writers to recognise and correct many errors which would otherwise go unnoticed except by the teacher's red pen. The sense of satisfaction created by a smart looking text undoubtedly enhances learning, or more particularly the willingness to learn, and many teachers have made much of the value of the word processor in this respect. Undoubtedly, there is truth in this view though there is a nagging worry for some teachers that too much attention may be paid to format and too little to content. As already outlined, however, we are here mainly concerned with the use of the word processor in the pre-writing and compositional stages of writing, the formative, thinking phase if you like, before final revisions and editing.

Consider first Figure 7.1, a transcript of a discussion between a small group of seven to eight-year-olds who have just read a poem by E.E. Cummings, 'Hist Whist' (from the Puffin anthology 'Merry Go Round').

Here young children are thinking aloud, expressing their responses to a poem which they have read and enjoyed but which also puzzles them. Sometimes they seem to be engaged in a collective monologue, at other times they interact. Later when given an opportunity to listen to the recording they were every bit as interested in what they had to say.

In much the same way as listening to a tape recording of a previous discussion the word processor offers the opportunity to throw out ideas and then to stand back and look at them. More important it offers an opportunity to move the words around the screen connecting them in a variety of ways, looking at different combinations and making comparisons. This process is not dissimilar to the technique of brainstorming where the teacher makes a lightning quick blackboard record of everything the children have said in a class discussion or where groups of children do it for themselves using small cards or squares of paper which may later be moved around and reconstructed into an ideas web for display on the wall.

A very good example of an ideas web can be seen on a publicity poster obtainable from IBM. A drawing of the sun placed in the centre of a web, the poster illustrates a wide

Figure 7.1: A Transcript of Children Reading 'Hist Whist'.

| | |
|---|---|
| Simon: | What does hob-a-nob mean? |
| Jenny: | Jumping. |
| Hazel: | Hob-a-nob means - hobs - |
| Jenny: | Like hopping. |
| Matthew: | Like skipping.. and sk.. |
| Hazel: | Hopping behind the witch or summat. |
| Various: | Mm..ssss |
| Matthew: | No.. hop out of the - pot. |
| Simon: | Little..(giggle) |
| Jenny: | Yeah. |
| Matthew: | Here the - green dancing devil devil devil devil whee..e..e. |
| Simon: | Yeah. |
| Hazel: | Could be - erm - the devil dancing round the pot or summat. |
| Jenny: | Yeah. |
| Matthew: | Yes, of course. |
| Simon: | Yeah. |
| Matthew: | Devil's dance. |
| Simon: | Devils dancing round the pot with snakes in it. |
| Hazel: | Yeah - and snakes all creeping out - up to the top. |
| Simon: | Mm - er like a woman that would - y'know that film the woman where snakes - |
| Hazel: | Yeah. |
| Matthew: | Yeah. |
| Jenny: | (Oh for she knows the devil oh the devil ouch - |
| Hazel: | I saw that.. at the pictures - |
| Jenny: | The devil oh the great green dancing devil, devil, devil wheese - what does that mean, then? |
| Hazel: | Well, I don't know. |
| Jenny: | The dancing.. the green devil dancing round her.. dancing round the pot. |
| Simon: | Yeah. |
| Hazel: | And she makes it all her own and everything - |
| Simon: | For she knows the devil ouch, the devil - ouch - |
| Hazel: | The snakes.. how she knows so it could - be - that - she.. |
| Jenny: | It could be the woman with snakes on her hair. |
| Simon: | I know that, I know that - something like somebody being caught by the devil. |
| Hazel: | Yeah. |
| Jenny: | Or someone's got a mind they're going to do something what the devil wishes 'em to do. |
| Hazel: | Yeah! |
| Matthew: | And the witch is like a devil is she.. she spells. |

range of interconnected concepts - people, places, ideas, things and events - all of which are directly related to the physical fact of the sun or associated with ideas represented by the sun.

Once children begin rearranging, discarding, classifying or connecting ideas, they have entered into the vital compositional stage of writing where coherent and cohesive sentences and paragraphs become important. This sorting out and shaping of the raw material must take place if a story or essay is to prove a worthwhile learning experience for the novice writer. Children who have been taught how to draw upon their own experiences will produce, individually and collectively, tons of raw material which they are then equally capable of organising and shaping toward a particular end, provided they do not have to enter too soon the linear or syntactic stage of writing in polished sentences.

Here is an example of what we mean. Three ten-year-olds have been visiting a local church and are pooling their information and personal impressions (spellings and punctuations have been corrected).

It's old
built in 15th century
There's graves outside
Inside is a font with a big lid on and a chain up to the ceiling
candles, pews, placards on the walls
old flags
Victorian
we drew a plan
a cross shape
like a boat
the vicar is Rev. P. Lindsey
a tomb
the stained glass window has got an angel on and
soldiers in the Great War
an apple tree at the back
and a wyche elm
on the wall there's a carving of a pig and a sheep in stone
confetti in the porch
it got burnt in 1876 the tower
the spire never got rebuilt
a map of Africa on a pillar some arrows
it smelt nice
it smelt funny
we do the nativity there at Christmas
a curtain at the back and some bell ropes
there's a gate and it hangs down at one side
the clock doesn't work

Immediately it will be seen that this information needs rearranging into some sort of order. Two headings which suggest themselves, for example, are

the church's interior
the church's exterior

Next, the historical sequence needs clarifying. How can it be both 15th century and Victorian? Where is the best place for information about the vicar? Or about the arrows on the map of Africa?

Once reorganisation has begun the need for additional information becomes apparent e.g. What is the name of the church? Whose flags are they? Why are there carvings of a pig and a sheep? And so on. There is absolutely no need, at this stage, for the information to be written in continuous prose; a data file of thoughtfully set out information with appropriate headings would be perfectly appropriate.

Many teachers will already be familiar with approaches to reading and writing which require children to organise and re-organise information they have learned or to handle text in more reflective ways. Appendix 2 provides a summary of activities usually referred to nowadays as DARTS (Directed Activities Related to Text) and which have now become essential techniques and strategies in the repertoire of teachers wishing to help children learn more effectively from the written word. Young readers may apply any of these techniques (e.g. underlining, labelling, sequencing, modelling) to texts on which they are currently working. DARTS promote a more active, reflective kind of reading by requiring children to interrogate and reorganise written information to useful ends. They require children to do rather more with texts than merely read them passively.

Similarly the word processor enables children to do things with their own texts using specific techniques for whatever purposes they have in mind e.g. deleting, inserting, reorganizing. Just as the techniques of DARTS need to be practised before children can really learn from such approaches to reading, so some techniques need to be learned if children are to be able to use a word processor effectively in their own writing.

Problems raised by the use of a word processor in a classroom are not just questions of keyboard skills but questions of computer management which will be helped or hindered by the extent of the hands on experience of both teachers and pupils. Below are some accounts taken from the reports of teachers participating in an MEP project investigating the use of the word processor in language arts teaching. They show different ways of tackling such practical problems as the structuring of activities to give pupils guidance and instruction; the integration of the use of the word processor with other kinds of learning; and the development of a style of classroom management which will cope with an, albeit embryonic, new environment for learning.

## SOME CASE STUDIES

### Teacher A

Introducing the word processor to young children requires some thought. As teachers we do not normally provide children with a tool - be it a pencil or a calculator - without first giving some guidance on the purposes for which it may be used. Conversely, giving children too much guidance can reduce their opportunities for learning.

A good introductory approach is to provide a dedicated word processor, say, a teletext emulator or a newspaper emulator. These programs have some of the facilities of word processors but provide specific contexts for their use:

- Teletext emulators allow text and pictures to be displayed on screen in a similar manner to Ceefax. Examples of these programs are ELECTRONIC NEWS, MIKEFAX and EDFAX.
- Newspaper emulators print out facsimile newspaper front pages containing information typed into the computer. Examples of these programs are FRONT PAGE and FLEET STREET EDITOR.

Effective use of these programs requires children first, to examine the programs' commercial counterparts to discern their style and form, and secondly, to adopt the appropriate style in their own writing. The contexts of these programs suggest aims and end products whilst the boundary conditions created by the various stylistic requirements provide the children with guidance for their writing.

Using dedicated word processors in this way will be attractive to the many primary schools which base their philosophies on experiential learning - learning by doing. In producing, for instance, a newspaper front page, children are learning about journalistic writing and, in our particular case, learning to use a limited set of word processing facilities built into the program. An approach to word processing along these lines will almost certainly be more successful in the primary school than one in which, for instance, the children complete sets of exercises. In an experiential approach word processing takes its proper place, as a means to achieving the end and not as an end in itself.

Many schools, however, may have to accept the fact that for the foreseeable future they will be unable to afford a full word processor which makes it even more urgent, in the meantime, to introduce whatever word processing software is currently and inexpensively available. It can be argued, anyway, that creative or original writing is difficult enough without the added problems of learning to use a new tool at the same time. This situation may be considerably eased by the introduction of a story writing program which, as a dedicated word processor, would act as a half-way house. Programs such as MICROSTORY and SWITCHIT offer plenty of opportunities for redrafting and for editing spellings and punctuation.

MICROSTORY helps children to write a story by providing a structure into which users put their own context while SWITCHIT does the same by providing pictures and requiring users to change the context. Children writing a story with either of these programs can save it on disc and recover it using the WORDWISE word processing program. If the children are introduced to the insertion and deletion facilities which represent the core of any word processing program, the successive drafts of the children's story may be corrected for punctuation and spelling and the expression examined for unnecessary repetitions, inconsistencies and faulty syntax.

As the children's experience widens, further facilities of the word processor, e.g. previewing and printing text and saving and loading text from disc can be introduced as needed. The powerful but often confusing facilities available in a word processing package, whilst benefitting the experienced user, cannot be said to be vital and need not be brought to the children's immediate attention.

Figure 7.2 reproduces the successive drafts of a story written by two ten-year-olds whose original story, draft 1, was written using SWITCHIT.

The points made in this section are best summarised as follows:

- The word processor is a resource, a writing tool which is only required when text is being created and edited for specific purposes. All children need access to one but not all the time.
- Primary children will learn to use a word processor more easily if it is introduced as a first-hand experience and is used to produce something tangible rather than merely used to progress through a series of exercises.
- Primary children do not need knowledge of all the facilities of a word processor. They can operate adequately on very few facilities, namely insertion and deletion, and can be shown further ones when needed.
- Dedicated word processors such as teletext and newspaper emulators provide a good first stage activity since they have context and purpose built in.

Figure 7.2: An Example of Work Using SWITCHIT and WORDWISE.

---

Nicola & Katy Draft 1

the olympic bike rider raced quickly along the racetrack.
he was coming to the final stretch, and when the rider pulled his back brake he nudged his nearest rider and caused him to fall into the nearby crowd.
the well kept bike swiftly cleared the corner with out a single mistake.
he looked over his shoulder, the rider could see only one rider behind him he realised he could win even though the rider nearby was rapidly catching up.
When the rider suddenly stumbled on a stone and the rider tried hard to keep his balence and has he began to regain his balence. a loud aplause broke out as the finishing flag went up for he had just won the race.

Nicola & Katy Draft 2

The Olympic bike rider raced quickly along the racetrack.
He was coming to the final stretch, and when the rider pulled his back brake he nudged his nearest rider and caused him to fall into the nearby crowd.
The well kept bike swiftly cleared the corner with out a single mistake.
He looked over his shoulder, the rider could see only one rider behind him he realised he could win even though the rider nearby was rapidly catching up.
When the rider suddenly stumbled on a stone and the ride. tried hard to keep his balance and as he began to regain his balance.
A loud applause broke out as the finishing flag went up for he had just won the race.

Nicola & Katy Draft 3

The olympic bike rider raced quickly along the racetrack.
He was coming to the final stretch, and when the rider pulled his back brake he nudged the nearest rider and caused him to fall into the nearby crowd.
The well kept bike swiftly cleared the corner with out a single mistake.
He looked over his shoulder, the leader could see only one biker behind him he realised he could win even though the rider nearby was rapidly catching up.
When the leader suddenly stumbled on a stone he tried hard to keep his balance and as he began to regain his balance.
A loud applause broke out as the finishing flag went up for he had just won the race.

Nicola & Katy    Draft 4

The olympic bike rider raced quickly along the racetrack.
He was coming to the final stretch, and when the rider pulled his back brake he nudged the nearest rider and caused him to fall into the nearby crowd.
The well kept bike swiftly cleared the corner with out a single mistake.
Suddenly the bike developed a puncture and he lost control. He fell into the crowd and was helpless.
Luckily his rescue team drove up in their van. They quickly changed his tyre. After he had got going and regained his balance he looked over his shoulder. The leader could see only one biker behind him he realised he could win even though his nearby rival was rapidly catching up.
When the leader suddenly stumbled on a stone he tried hard to keep his balance and he began to regain his balance.
A loud applause broke out as the finishing flag went up for he had just won the race.

Nicola & Katy    Draft 5

The Olympic bike rider raced quickly along the racetrack.
He was coming to the final stretch, and when the rider pulled his back brake he nudged him and caused him to fall into the nearby crowd.The well kept bike swiftly cleared the corner with out a single mistake.
Suddenly the bike developed a puncture and he lost control. He fell into the crowd and was helpless. Luckily his rescue team drove up in their van. They quickly changed his tyre.After he had got going and regained his balance he looked over his shoulder. The leader could see only one biker behind him he realised he could win even though his nearby rival was rapidly catching up. The leader suddenly stumbled on a stone he tried hard to keep his balance. A loud applause broke out as the finishing flag went up for he had won race.

---

- Programs that help children to produce stories which can be fed into a word processor for refining represent a useful second stage activity since they provide beginners with support yet allow greater freedom to more confident users.

Teacher B

This account describes a self instruction course for introducing pupils to WORDWISE PLUS.

The course is, in essence, a series of WORDWISE text files which mix short explanations with instructions for simple tasks. The instructions are coloured green so that the pupils' responses in white will be distinctive. The course began with a lead lesson demonstrating how the computer is a useful tool for thinking with. First a clumsy, ill thought out sentence was dictated by the teacher and written on the blackboard by a pupil. The sentence was then revised by the teacher with the pupil making all the changes on the blackboard. Since

Figure 7.3: An Example of 'Insult Tennis'.

```
John is fat.
John is fast.
John is not fast.
John is not bad looking.
John is really bad looking.
Peter is really bad looking.
Peter is really cool.
If Peter is really cool I am a banana.
John is a banana.
```

Figure 7.4: A Sample Text File for Children to Use.

```
WRITE ON

It is time you used skills you have been learning to do a
proper piece of writing, and perhaps get it printed out. Below
are three sets of outline notes for a story. Choose the one
you think most interesting and get rid of the others by
deleting them.

Next, build up the notes into a fully developed story in
proper sentences.

1. Man collecting in street - label says 'Blind' - kind lady
throws 10p in cap - misses - rolls in gutter - man picks it up
- lady protests - 'Sorry, missus' - wrong label - should be
'Deaf and Dumb'.

2. Sun and wind argue which is stronger - traveller passes -
agree whichever makes him take coat off is winner - wind fails
- sun succeeds.

3. Convict escaped 2 pm - over prison wall - across gardens
over roof tops - fire brigade called - convict drenched -
surrendered 3 pm.
```

rubbing out was forbidden the board was soon covered with a thicket of crossings out and insertions. Once this stage had been reached the same process was demonstrated on WORDWISE which impressed the pupils considerably.

At a later stage, after explanation of how to load the first self instruction file which shows them how to use basic features of the keyboard, the pupils played a game of 'Insult Tennis'. This is designed for two players and requires the use of insertion and deletion procedures to change any insult or compliment previously inserted. A typical exchange between two players is given in Figure 7.3.

Another text file takes users through a set of proof correction exercises after which pupils are given scope for using the word processor to write at greater length. They are offered three plots in fragmented form and asked to choose one for expanding into a full story. The skeleton plots are about 30 words long and a helpful target for the completed story is 200 words. Pupils can use the word count at the top of the EDIT MODE screen to keep track, a procedure which is not as mechanical as it may at first sound since it serves not only to get pupils going but also to discourage them from too speedy solutions. The story often develops its own momentum long before the target figure is reached so that the target becomes irrelevant. Figure 7.4 shows a sample text file giving story writing instruction.

Teacher C

The compilation of a guidebook to a local area is not an original idea but it is an excellent way of drawing upon pupils' own knowledge and experience and of providing both an audience and a purpose for their writing. It can be consulted by other children and their families for information about where to go or about what is on locally. It also offers an opportunity for the writers to communicate, at the same time, personal information or a particular point of view.

WORDWISE proved an ideal tool for composing the text of the guidebook and for giving it a professional finish, while the idea of the guidebook proved equally effective for giving pupils first hand experience of using the program. In addition the use of WORDWISE provides the class not only with the text of a booklet but also with a set of data files which can be consulted on the screen and which can easily be updated.

Without the use of WORDWISE there is no doubt that the class would have completed the task much more quickly. Progress was in general extremely slow though some children were able to work quite quickly on their own sections. The teacher herself was a novice so far as computers were concerned and could not have anticipated the problems which would arise nor the amount of time required.

Nevertheless the time spent initially on discussing layout and trying different effects on the screen proved invaluable. Once an agreed format for information had been reached each child was able to concentrate on content and on the acquisition of word processing skills. This approach is in fact the exact opposite of Teacher B's who, as a far more experienced computer user, was able to devise a set of preliminary exercises. Undoubtedly children compiling the booklet would have benefited from such exercises but the learning experience of proceeding by trial and error proved to have compensatory advantages. Gradually, for example, a list of rules was drawn up after careful consultation of the WORDWISE handbook each time a problem arose. The activity also generated an extremely rich language environment in which children discussed spontaneously such issues as spelling, syntax, stylistic unity, accuracy or appropriateness of content, punctuation and choice of vocabulary.

Though progress proved slow in the first stages the children's commitment to what they were doing never faltered and on many occasions the quicker ones would offer assistance to less skilful but equally determined pupils. There can be no doubt about the quality of the learning even under, or perhaps because of, such difficult conditions. So far as the teacher is concerned the risks involved sometimes wore her ragged but the accelerated and accumulated learning, not only about word processing but also about a new style of class management, proved ultimately satisfying and worthwhile.

Figure 7.5 reproduces some examples of the children's work in progress. They have not been edited but demonstrate the care children will take when faced with the challenge to be experts.

The interesting mixture of guidebook information and personal knowledge has in fact provided the basis for an amusing 'alternative guide' to Widnes expressing very much the youngsters' point of view.

Teacher D

Another natural activity for incorporating the use of word processing is the writing and editing of a magazine or 'Electronic Newspaper'. Much of the initial work was done, of course, away from the word processor itself e.g. information gathering; tape recorded interviews; first drafts; jokes; inventing problems to be solved; illustrations.

Once children were ready to use WORDWISE they had first to come to terms with one of its peculiarities. When the user writes text on the screen WORDWISE employs a line width of 40 characters. The advantage of this is that the characters are larger and easier to work with than the smaller ones on an 80 character screen. The disadvantage of this is that because text is usually printed out with 80 characters

Figure 7.5: Examples of Children's Guide Book Writing.

---

WIDNES MARKET

Widnes market is a good place for you to go shopping. It has got lots of good things in store for you like dresses, trainers and sweet stalls. The market is only open on Monday, Friday and Saturday. Also it has got more shops around it like a chip shop, a flower shop, a computer shop and a job centre. How to get there - get a bus to Widnes Town Hall, then you will get off the bus outside a pub, the Game Bird. Then just walk round the corner where you will see a big building with a sign pointing to the market.
Buses 12, 14, 15 and the H20.

LIVERPOOL

Liverpool has got a continuous row of shops. They are: C+A, Marks and Spencers, Thorntons, Boots, Toy and Hobby, A Photograph booth, Sweet shops, Mother care, British Home Stores, Chelsea Girl, Shoe shops, Kids Talk, Girls Talk and many more. Also there are two cathedrals. They are the Anglican Cathedral and the metropolitan cathedral. Liverpool has a lot of fancy restaurants. Liverpool is a very popular place. Liverpool has got a place for handicapped children.
How to get there -
Trains - you can get a train at any local station.
Buses - You can get the H20 and the H21.

LIVERPOOL AIRPORT

Speke

Liverpool Airport has a balcony from which you can get a beautiful view of the River Mersey. It has a small airport nestling on the banks of the Mersey, in the south end of the city of Liverpool. It has a modern runway and the length of it is approximately 1 and half miles. Liverpool Airport is not normally ever used. It is only used in the cases of inclement weather. Because of this there are a lot of flight diversions from Manchester. Also in the event of accidents to air traffic.
The airport lies in the beautiful surroundings of the River Mersey estuary. Anybody visiting the airport could spend a pleasant day there.
How to get there - it is quite easy to get there from Halebank. If you turn into Halegate Road and carry on into Town Lane which will take you through Hale Village you then go via Hale Road which takes you into Speke. You then turn right into Western Avenue which brings you to Route 7. You then turn

```
left and this road takes you straight to the main gates.
Telephone:  051 494 0066

SHIRDLEY PARK AND CONTON COLLIERY

A 20 minute drive from Widnes Centre. It is a pleasurable
place for football, cricket etc.
Its facilities are parks, rides, and swings, as well as
climbing frames etc.
A small zoo is also included in the facilities. The Wheelhouse
golfcourse is right in front of a 17th century inn where you
can go for a drink and a bite to eat. Admittance is free which
is very good. But on the golfcourse you hire clubs etc. for
5.00 an hour.
Five minutes down the road is Cronton Colliery.
First you put on your 'gear'. Then collect 2 tokens and make
your way to the shaft. On the bottom of the pit your guide
will show you, how the pit used to work, and how it works
today.
After your tour you can go into the canteen.
Admission
£2.50 for adults
£1.50 for children and O.A.Ps.
```

---

per line the final product does not look quite what the user expected. What you get is not the same as what you thought you had put on the screen. Some pupils got into deep water when they attempted a fancy layout simply because they had not anticipated the change in typescript. The simple solution is to use WORDWISE's LL embedded command to set the printer to print out only 40 characters per line. A more flexible solution emerged later when one pupil, designated by the others as the layout and art editor, began to learn a little more about formatting and the use of previewing. By this means he learned to juggle with the widths of the columns and eventually took over the presentation of all the texts produced by his group.

This very practical division of labour is, of course, the way it would be done on a professional magazine. Just one practical experience such as this took them to the heart of the newspaper revolution wrought by Eddie Shah, and gave them far more understanding of what that revolution means than all the television news commentary put together.

## SOME REFLECTIONS

The effective use of a word processor in the classroom depends upon some degree of familiarity with the keyboard.

This can be achieved by trial and error (on the part of both teachers and pupils) or by a sequence of introductory tasks and exercises. The latter course will be preferable to some teachers and quite apart from its efficiency, it does offer additional opportunities for explicit language learning e.g. paying attention to punctuation, spelling, sentence structure. The experience of the teacher working by trial and error and learning alongside the pupils, was reported in the Times Educational Supplement under the ironic title 'Will it be my turn in a fortnight, Miss?'. The article draws attention to another problem almost as important as the acquisition of keyboard skills and that is the general problem of the classroom management of computer assisted learning. Whichever course is pursued, however, and despite all the difficulties, teachers who have introduced word processing into their classrooms seem to agree on the advantages it brings to both learners and teachers. For learners it:

- enhances their perceptions of themselves as 'real writers'.
- gives their text a better public image.
- brings their writing closer to public forms of communication and adult models.
- teaches them how to edit their own work.
- gives them a new perspective on spelling and punctuation errors.
- enables them to reflect on the thinking which goes on behind the writing.
- makes it easier for them to share their work with others.
- encourages and facilitates collaborative writing.
- gives them control over the pace and direction of their own learning.
- helps them adopt an appropriately self-critical distance from their writing.
- encourages experimentation and risk taking.
- provides a focus for group discussion.
- presents content free challenges to which pupils can respond in their own ways.

For teachers it:

- permits them to spend more time on individual supervision and tuition.
- directs and controls the work of small groups.
- makes easier the provision of audiences and purposes for writing.
- gives teachers a store of information (e.g. successive re-drafts) on children's writing and thinking processes.

A cautionary note sounded by some teachers is the danger of pupils becoming too concerned with the format and the appearance of their writing and less thoughtful about its content. Another is that an excess of revising and editing may lead to self-consciousness and a lack of spontaneity while a third note of warning is that too much insistence on collaborative writing could detract from the privacy also necessary for the completion of satisfying and successful writing. None of these observations need deter teachers who are already used to an interactive, personal relationship with young writers. Over-concern with smart appearances need be no more detrimental than the discouragement engendered by poor handwriting. Revising and editing should always be discussed sensitively with the child and not required as automatic responses, while collaborative writing offers so many advantages and cumulative gains that the children can be relied upon to make their own demands for privacy when they feel they need it.

The final point is a hackneyed one but nonetheless true: if the word processor is used without any real learning purposes or teaching objectives then it will be no better an aid to thoughtful writing than a new ball pen. It is the ability of the word processor to allow children to concentrate on refining what they want to say which makes the machine so exciting. If the arrival of the cheap calculator gave teachers and their pupils the opportunity to access the mathematics behind the calculations the word processor, in the same way, allows them to pay attention to the thinking behind the writing.

Chapter Eight

# 'IT MAKES YOU THINK!'

## THE STATE OF THE ART

In an edition of February 1985, the Times reported a news item under the headline, 'Primary School Sells Its Pedal Car To Buy Computer'. In order to raise the money for a computer a school in Devon had decided to sell a comparatively rare pedal car, made by Austin in 1960. It had obviously given delight in the school playground for many years and it seems regrettable that the children should have had to 'put away childish things' so young. Common sense, of course, acknowledges it to have been a good way of enabling children to make decisions about their own learning whilst at the same time preserving a collector's piece. It also emphasises a home truth: technology requires cash.

It has, however, during the first half of the 1980s, been relatively easy for primary teachers to make a start on the use of computers. The support provided by MEP together with the excellent basic design of the BBC computer have proved invaluable, while the climate of enthusiasm and the exchange of ideas has sustained committed teachers and converted many more. True, there has never been very much language arts software available but the incidental gains for language development through the use of programs not specifically linguistic (e.g adventure games, simulations and even databases) have been very welcome. In some schools SPACEX, for example, has generated more than enough talking and writing for the average super-teacher to handle in three crowded terms! Equally, the negotiating skills necessary, simply to manage the use of the machine by one class of children, form a sociolinguistic network all of their own.

In Chapter One we stated that a growing number of English teachers had enthusiastically involved themselves in the use of computers but, now that the euphoric stage is over and whilst conviction remains strong, there are signs that teachers are beginning to look for consolidation and practical provision for the future. The first NATE conference to include a commission on computer technology was, appropriately enough, given the general title, 'Tomorrow's World'.

In the succeeding chapters we have tried to demonstrate that the microcomputer, far from being the sole property of the scientist and mathematician, has much to offer any teacher of the language arts and that language programs can be far more imaginative than tables testers and spelling bees.

Teachers unfamiliar with the use of computers in schools continue to believe that the computer's educational role is that of a teaching machine. Oddly enough, this is the role which the computer is least well-adapted to take. It seems to make an ideal partner in the learning process but proves a particularly dull and undemanding taskmaster.

We have tried to show some ways in which the computer can make positive contributions to language development in a catalytic rather than an instructional way. These may be summarised as follows:

- It can supply additional language experiences for children. Two examples of this are (i) the opportunity for discussion when playing an adventure game and (ii) the unfamiliar narrative experience of writing one.
- It can supply aid to children in an existing area of language work e.g. the framework provided by the program MICROSTORY for children's story-writing.
- It can allow children to play with words and ideas within a poetic framework e.g. WORDPLAY and POEMWRITER.
- It can add a new dimension to otherwise familiar projects and, by providing a new tool, can suggest new project areas offering new opportunities for language development e.g. DIET and FACTFILE.
- It can supply a situation in which the children write in a specific form with unfamiliar but challenging constraints e.g. FRONT PAGE and ELECTRONIC NEWS.
- It can lure children into unfamiliar territory, inject a sense of drama and deepen their learning experiences in the manner of WULFSTAN'S WORDHOARD, for instance.
- It can act as a tool for investigating small but important areas of language use. This kind of program, which is gaining more and more credence, may be likened to a magnifying glass as used by a biologist to discern greater detail. In a similar way, the computer can reveal nuances of language. Examples of programs which do this are DEVELOPING TRAY and SWITCHIT.
- It can be used as a word processor which must be

> the most exciting creative tool for writing since the invention of pen and ink. By lessening the sheer fatigue of redrafting the word processor makes it possible for more children than ever before to become 'writers' in every sense of the word. If English teachers use the computer for nothing else they owe it to their charges to allow them the creative freedom which the word processor offers. A word processor is the ideal 'open program' for language development.

We have tried to sustain through the book a practical approach to the use of computers and have accepted the limitations of the classroom horizon. Nevertheless, from time to time, even the most enthusiastic computer users look beyond that horizon as they instinctively discern wider personal and social implications of computer technology. Working hard to demonstrate the positive factors goes hand in hand with efforts to allay the negative ones. Evaluating the pluses and minuses of computer innovation is almost as difficult as assessing a piece of original writing done by a child. Sophisticated assessment schedules are all well and good but a better way of getting to the heart of the matter is simply to make a list of three achievements in a child's work and then a list of three constraints. Similarly the gains for language development offered by computers need to be viewed against the disadvantages.

We suggest a collective list of pitfalls based on the views of primary teachers who have contributed to MEP curriculum development projects.

- It is easier to make software which controls children's responses rather than software which is controlled by the children.
- It is easier to make the teaching fit the computer rather than the computer fit the teaching.
- It is easier to allow the computer to manipulate the children through routines than it is to use it to broaden their linguistic experiences.
- It is easier to steamroller the organisation of computers in the classroom than it is to observe and incorporate the ways in which children actually use computers.
- It is easier to reduce literacy teaching to a set of routines than it is to enhance it as a comprehensive, intellectual ability.
- It is easier to 'teach' computer technology as a separate subject than it is to integrate it into the rest of the curriculum.
- It is easier to blame computers than it is to blame

human beings. (Ask anyone tendering an incorrect bill!)

If this sounds a little like Frank Smith's famous list of 'Twelve ways to Make Learning to Read Difficult' then it is a pleasure to be in the company of such a distinguished educational thinker who is equally excited and cautious about the future for computer technology and literacy.

A more general anxiety has been expressed by Daniel Chandler:

> Anyone who values creativity cannot fail to be disturbed by the fact that computers are appearing in schools at a time when there is a growing convergence of outlook among educators and the public that the main goal of education is to develop the concrete operational skills of technical reason coupled with functional, utilitarian 'skills' in language. The current reification of technique reflects the belief that the only important learning is that which can be precisely described in quantifiable terms ('the Basics'): it is a value system which champions instrumental reason at the expense of human values. And the computer is a powerful tool for technocrats who think like this; it takes no imagination and little effort to make the computer function as a monitor of mechanical operations.

It is worth noting here that the slogan 'Back to Basics', usually taken to be a rallying cry for the inculcation of 'real' teaching and 'real' learning, in practice adds up to little more than a concern for spelling, punctuation and formal grammar exercises which concentrate on the surface features of written language rather than the deeper sources of language development. Young writers need to be taught how to generate and connect their sentences from deeper levels of thought and intention; no amount of editorial skills teaching (the supposed 'Basics') will provide a route to the thinking and planning stages of language production.

David Dillon, another advocate of the imaginative use of computers for language arts teaching, alerts teachers to seven dangers, some of which reflect questions raised in the Connecticut Delphi Study:

- Will the use of computers limit our notions and practice of literacy?
- Who is in charge? i.e. whom does the technology empower?
- Where do imagination and feelings fit into the emerging cognitive and technological view of knowledge and learning?
- What social disadvantages will be reinforced by

unequal access to computer assisted learning?
- How do we guard against ignorant or fearful computer policies directed by educational administrations?
- How do we take into account the children's perspectives?
- When are we going to stop treating computers as a special issue?

Taken together all these doubts, dangers and pitfalls add up to an impressive case for the prosecution and are more than sufficient to inspire a new Luddite rebellion.

At the beginning of this chapter we drew attention to a primary school where the children had voted to sell their antique plaything in order to join the technological revolution. Some readers will also be familiar with Peter Dickinson's novel 'The Weathermonger' in which the world, overcome by technological and nuclear disaster, has returned to a new dark age in which any form of machinery is regarded as evil and destroyed forthwith. The children at the centre of the story are trying to re-unite themselves with their parents. They travel about the country in a vintage Rolls Royce, always in danger from marauding bands of machine-wreckers. It is difficult to know which is more ironic: the facts of the Taunton primary school or the fiction of John Dickinson's novel.

One thing which seems certain is that if teachers wish to retain some influence on the future lives of their pupils they will need to come to terms in heart and mind with the technology now on offer. Admittedly, the most powerful forces in computer technology operate in business, commercial and military spheres; education being a very poor relative indeed. For those who are inclined to be pessimistic about what teachers can do, it is worth remembering that over 2000 years ago Plato sounded a warning against an earlier technology which, he thought, would have drastic consequences for mankind. It would, he said, destroy memory and weaken the mind. It was unable to explain itself and, furthermore, it was inhuman, pretending to establish outside the mind what can only exist inside the mind. It was a thing, a manufactured product, unresponsive, passive and artificial. If all this sounds like a critique of communication and information technology in the 1980s, it is in fact a critique of the invention of writing by which means Ancient Greece changed from an oral tradition to a literate culture. Writing, we now regard as an essential expression of thought and feelings, a preserver of the highest human values. It is the very medium through which we can get in touch with the mind of Socrates whose wisdom we can know only through the writings of Plato.

What short to medium term view then can teachers take and what courses of action are likely to prove worthwhile?

## THE FUTURE

### The Pupils' View

It is a brave individual who is willing to predict the future concerning computers. Technology has a disconcerting habit of turning science fiction into domestic fact; yesterday's scientific instruments become today's playthings.

In the novel, 'The Crocus List', Gavin Lyall writes the following dialogue:

> 'Can we record it?' Maxim asked.
>
> 'YOU might be able to; it takes me half an hour to set up that blasted thing and then it usually gets the wrong programme. They ought to give away a ten-year-old child with every video machine. And every other sort of machine they're swamping us with these days.'

Many teachers readily admit that their pupils are 'better at it' than they are when it comes to computer technology and a wise course of action may well be to find out much more about how children understand and interpret their experience of computers.

When asked to suggest some things which the computer could do, one group of children, who have had plenty of experience using a computer, made the following list:

- It makes you think!
- It can prepare you for other computers you might meet in any job you might get.
- It can help you to draw pictures.
- It can help you to read and write better. (The word processor was pointed to in this context.)
- It can teach you languages. (In this context the children referred to various programs which, while purporting to teach foreign languages, were merely translating any word typed into the computer rather in the way of an automatic translation dictionary. When this was pointed out to the children they responded with the opinion that the computer was more fun.)
- It can help you do maths more easily. (Many of the children foresaw this as being detrimental to their education; the computer doing more meant that they would do less and so learn less.)
- It can teach history by asking you questions and giving you the answers if you don't know them. (This is reminiscent of the earlier point about

foreign languages; it is hardly surprising to come across this opinion from a ten-year-old since there seem to be many teachers who, sadly, share his opinion.)
- It can help you to design things. (When pressed for more details, the girl who suggested this pointed to the examples of maps and books which had been made during the recent project using WULFSTAN'S WORDHOARD. i.e. objects which had been designed away from the computer but had been inspired by it.)

The children were then asked to suggest some of the things which they believed a computer couldn't do. Their suggestions were:

- Maths. It can only give you the answer, it can't help you to do it. (They did not regard using Logo for constructing various mathematical shapes to be part of mathematics at all!)
- It can't think for you it can only do what it is programmed to do. (Quite a sophisticated view for ten-year-olds.)
- It can't teach you handwriting. (Many of the group were keen calligraphers.)
- PE and Games. ('Well, it can't, can it?')
- It can't dream. ('I can, asleep or awake.')

Another group was asked to consider a small primary school, say of 120 children, and suggest what the provision of computers might be by the year 2000. Of the 30 children asked, 17 of them thought that there would be between 6 and 10 computers throughout the school, 5 thought there would be less, 3 thought more and 5 had no opinion. Only one child thought that there would be a computer supplied for each child.

The children were asked how they thought the computers would be distributed in the school. Most thought that there would be a computer room to be used by one class at a time. It was suggested by some children that there would be a computer supplied between two children which would be used for all their work instead of exercise books.

Some suggested that there would be no school at all. All work would be done at home on computers linked to a large computer directing the operations.

The children were asked what subjects the computer would mainly be used for in the year 2000. They unanimously regarded this to be mathematics and science but well over half of the children mentioned English or writing in their answer. Often stated was the idea that the computer would do so much for the children that there would, in fact, be very little for them to do at all!

The future may well see children carrying around their personal Dynabooks which may be in total control of their education. It may not. Let us hope the future is not as chilling as one ten-year-old foresees it to be:

> I think computers will gradually outgrow themselves. Children will not need to know much and they will rely on computers so much that they will not know how to build any more computers. Therefore everything mechanical will disintegrate. By the year 3500 the people on earth will be like their ancestors in 1800.

Read another child's words:

Tomorrow is the future
Tomorrow is next year.
But blink your eyes
And open them
And there's the future, here.
Philip Waters

The boy who wrote that 20 years ago for a Dunstable school poetry anthology may well have children of his own now. The poem was triggered by the cover of a long forgotten science fiction thriller but it seems almost to have been written about microcomputers today.

## The Teacher's View

The combination of modern information technology and communications makes a formidable force for cultural and educational change. None of us are unaffected by it and we are all challenged not only to adopt new techniques but also to re-think traditional notions of language and learning. Changes seem to be occurring at all levels and each teacher must respond to, and interpret, them in his or her own classroom practice. At the level of teaching content, new perspectives on knowledge and information are challenging the teacher's conventional role as provider, whilst at the level of teaching method new developments in communication technology coupled with new social attitudes are challenging the ways in which teachers have traditionally related (or been related by the school system) to their pupils. Both of these in turn are creating a pressure for changes in classroom management, curricular thinking and educational style.

If, however, we are to take seriously David Dillon's warning about not making computers a special issue then we should put them very firmly in their place and conclude this book not with the subject of computers themselves but with some guidelines for language and learning, the twin concerns with which we started Chapter One. What seems to be necessary now for teachers who wish to move purposefully into tomorrow's classroom is a modest syllabus or programme of self-help. Instead of lurching forward with each new idea advertised in the latest editions of educational computing magazines, a programme of action research and personal involvement as a fellow learner in children's learning will give more confident insights. A programme of action research could be drawn up along the following lines:

- Observing how children think and reflecting on the processes underlying such activities as, for example, solving problems, writing stories, making decisions, planning actions.
- Studying far more closely the role of language in learning and thinking, and adopting structured as well as inventive approaches to teaching the language arts. It is this combination of structure and invention which so often generates the creativity.
- Reassessing from the learner's point of view the learning environment in the classroom. This will probably involve the teacher not just in directing the children's learning, but in sharing it, using information resources available for their own studies as well as those of their pupils.
- Being prepared for considerable changes in teaching style necessitated by resource-based learning.
- Developing a range of strategies for promoting and guiding different kinds of classroom talk.
- Recognising the strength of investigative and experiential learning and being ready to move each child on to the next appropriate stage.

Many teachers in the past ten or fifteen years have accomplished much in some or all of these areas but the changes have been hard-won. What computer technology offers is a resource which will help the teacher accomplish classroom changes which are long overdue. Used in the service of such a programme as the one just outlined the computer is very effectively put in its place as a tool for language and learning rather than a threat.

The argument that all these aims could be accomplished without the computer is a persuasive one but deliberately to ignore the computer's existence would be as foolish as imagining that previous generations of children could have been taught in school without access to dictionaries, textbooks or writing materials. For teachers to ignore any new technology, especially one for which the younger generation feels such affinity, would be a perverse impoverishment of the learning environment in schools. Teachers, on the other hand, who are prepared to welcome technology into the classroom, alongside literature, music and the arts, stand a good chance of enriching that environment provided they and their pupils are in control.

## REFERENCES

Lyall, G. (1980) The Crocus List (Hodder and Stoughton).

Appendix One

# A CONSIDERATION OF SOME OF THE WAYS IN WHICH COMPUTER TECHNOLOGY AFFECTS THE DEVELOPMENT OF LANGUAGE AND LEARNING

The opening discussions of the working party were concerned with establishing an agreed frame of reference in which observations and proposals could be made. The term 'skills' in the original formulation of the brief was rejected since it begged too many questions. If features of teaching and learning were to be itemised it was felt that terms such as language 'behaviour', learning 'strategies', and teaching 'styles' would be more appropriate. The phrase 'language development' was recognised as a compendium in which enlightened principles and retrograde practice could continue to flourish side by side as they always have done in English education.

Despite disclaimers and scepticism about terminology it was nevertheless felt that a number of important, positive and encouraging insights about language development and school learning are being demonstrated in the practice of a growing number of teachers in primary and secondary schools. The fact that lip-service is generally paid to the new orthodoxies about language and learning may be taken as a sign of success, not in implementing change but in creating a platform from which change may be brought about on a wider scale.

The present document cannot be a comprehensive statement about the role of computer technology in language development and the linguistic elements of learning; it sets out three areas of shared interests and concern and proceeds in the belief that they are important enough to merit sustained attention over the next three years. The general aim is not so much to justify and promote the use of computer technology per se as to recognise the achievements already made in the teaching of the language arts and to consider ways in which the computer technology might help to consolidate these achievements and enable the language curriculum to respond effectively and imaginatively to the demands of the 1990s.

Three areas of special concern were identified:

- The classroom environment and staff development.
- Designing, choosing and evaluating software for language development.
- The interrelationship of language, home and school.

## THE CLASSROOM ENVIRONMENT AND STAFF DEVELOPMENT

Computer assisted learning is as much about the ways in which we use language as it is about the ways in which we use technology. Regardless of the qualities (good or bad) of individual software, the use of the computer will reflect the teacher's own educational attitudes and be constrained by the prevailing environment for learning. Consequently, there are certain PRECONDITIONS that teachers of the language arts need to fulfil before they can implement the use of computers to any real advantage.

Some major preconditions are:

- Some progress in the establishment of resource-based learning (e.g. the provision of teacher produced materials geared to a particular class; the availability of a tape recorder etc.)
- A commitment to the value of children's talk in a variety of learning contexts (this would include the teacher's own style of talking to pupils).
- An informed understanding of the nature and functions of language in human society (e.g. some knowledge of modern linguistics and a willingness to investigate language in context).
- Experience in the supervision of different kinds of group work.
- The provision of opportunities for individual learning and one-to-one contact between pupils and the teacher.

Even when an individual teacher is thinking along the lines suggested here, the placing of just one word processor in the classroom will make considerable demands on his/her personal flexibility, resourcefulness and perseverance. Two curriculum constraints are particularly pressing:

- Lack of time in an already overcrowded curriculum: a resolution to do less but much better is one way forward.
- Lack of space in classrooms that are ill-designed for new styles of teaching and learning.

The working party's view is that a very special kind of in-service support is necessary here that will combine the management of classroom learning with informed professional judgement about language and computers. One approach might be the provision of guidelines to enable teachers to practise successfully a tri-partite division of time in which one third of their attention is devoted to class teaching, one third to group work and one third to individual learning. This would lead to making decisions about the deployment not only of the computer but of all classroom resources. A rule of thumb, such as the one given here, has the advantage of simplifying the process of change by providing a clear perspective for the teacher's own role in classroom learning. The success of in-service support designed specifically for curriculum change would depend not only on DES funding but also on close association with LEA advisers and the necessary involvement of senior school management. By making it possible for teachers to incorporate computer technology into their daily practice we would in fact provide an excellent opportunity for monitoring necessary non-technological changes, particularly in the secondary curriculum.

## DESIGNING, CHOOSING AND DEVELOPING SOFTWARE

One advantage to be gained from a clear view of classroom management (or the management of language arts lessons) is that teachers begin to formulate more precisely their resource needs. If, for example, teachers assess their responsibilities in terms of class teaching, group learning and individual supervision, available software can be initially assessed in terms of its usefulness to any one of these approaches.

So far as software development is concerned it is recommended by the working party that local groups should be established for which the MINIMUM requirement would be:

- A teacher-leader with expertise in language development.
- A professional programmer.
- A software designer who may or may not be a practising teacher but who should have a background in education.

Such teams should concern themselves with software developments now and in the near future. Attention could be focussed on collaborative learning activities and the ways these may be fostered by word processing, simulations, the use of information handling packages and the implications of speech generation and recognition (particularly in the area of special needs).

Concern was expressed, however, that the lack of information about what is available makes the choice of software a hit and miss affair. It was therefore proposed that two or three serving teachers (possibly Teacher Fellows) be appointed with a national responsibility for collecting local teacher group reviews and case studies of software throughout Britain, for collating that information and disseminating it to all interested bodies and individuals. The service would be comprehensive and up to date and would regularly feature teachers' own evaluations, commissioned on a professional basis.

## INTERRELATIONSHIP OF LANGUAGE, HOME AND SCHOOL

What has been recommended so far is a new initiative in in-service provision which would effectively combine resource production, classroom support and action research. It is not envisaged as something new in itself but rather as a renewal and redeployment of existing resources. Despite the growing awareness that the language development continuum is not restricted to the school environment, a strategy has yet to be designed and implemented that would draw together home and school. The working party has become increasingly convinced that the link between home and school is a central issue in the future of community educational provision in the language curriculum.

The general interest in computer technology, both within and beyond the school could be harnessed in a new partnership of teachers, parents and pupils. This would make possible a more coherent framework for the language curriculum in which all could learn together. Through this traditional home/school barriers could be broken down and new links forged between institutionalised school learning and experience of the world outside. In this context the computer would serve as catalyst whilst teachers would become facilitators of shared learning in the community. An example could best illustrate what is being proposed.

Using a database program, parent, pupil and teacher groups could be set up (as an evening class for example) to survey the knowledge, skills and interests evident in the local community. This could constitute not only a computer education project but also a useful piece of market research on behalf of adult education providers in the community. It would give recognition to parents' own expertise and interests whilst enabling teachers and parents to work together with pupils in an educational context.

It seems preferable to forge new links in a purposeful way such as this rather than trying to get parents (as parents) into school in order to persuade them to the school's point of view. The database would itself have value and could be extended into areas of other local information and local history. However, more importantly perhaps, in the process of creating it there could conceivably occur subtle changes in how pupils, parents and teachers perceive themselves in an educational context and ultimately alter the ways in which they act in relation to each other. The computer provides an opportunity for parents to work directly on educational projects which, provided the partnership is an equal one, would widen the curriculum and bring a new element into the classroom. Ostensibly the examples given may be more appropriate to history teaching or social studies but the sociolinguistic interest of such a venture will be readily acknowledge by teachers of the language arts whose awareness of the role of language in learning and the wider context of language use would have been nurtured in the kind of in-service framework proposed earlier.

This paper reports discussion which started with what the working party considered modest proposals for consolidating significant developments in the teaching of the language arts through the use of computer technology; they ended with a recognition that computers could also create networks, both human and electronic which would have considerable potential for forging home school links and for giving community education a much wider and more exciting perspective; a perspective on the language curriculum that could with some justice be called 'a language for life'.

A Report Made at the Cambridge Conference, 1985.

Appendix Two

# DIRECTED ACTIVITIES RELATED TO TEXT

## VARIETIES OF TEXTS

The difference between reading fiction and non-fiction is deeply rooted in the secondary curriculum. It is a distinction that has traditionally distinguished the work of English teachers from that of other colleagues, whether in Humanities of Sciences, and it frequently expresses itself one way or another in the declared reading preferences of young readers. Without necessarily prejudging issues raised by the linguistic and psychological differences it is nevertheless possible to make a preliminary classification of texts encountered by pupils in the classroom. They are:

- Narrative. Either fictional or non-fictional plus commentary.
- Expository. Information, argument and explanation presented in a variety of non-narrative forms.
- Instructional. Directive prose that frequently uses sequences.

It should also be observed that some texts may present a combination of any of these. An expository text, for example, may contain an anecdotal narrative.

## WHAT IS A DART?

DARTS initially demand a careful analysis of the content and structure of a text in order to anticipate learning difficulties or to identify specific opportunities for a deeper level of learning than might occur in the normally passive, receptive mode of reading. Critical insights gained by textual analysis should then inform an imaginative presentation of the text and give direction to specific reading activities. Pupils should be helped to achieve the following aims or purposes:

- Find information or recognise specific features.
- Learn from the way in which information or content is organised and presented.
- Make informed decisions and judgements about what they have read and use information for specific ends.

## TEXTUAL ANALYSIS

Textual analysis involves some or all of the following factors:

- Vocabulary. Identifying verbal or conceptual difficulties (e.g. specialist nomenclature or specialist use of common words).
- Grammar. Recognising sentence structure that might be confusing or ambiguous.
- Overall structure. Noting connections between sentences, relationships between paragraphs.
- Visual layout. Assessing use and value of complementary diagrams or tables.

## DART TECHNIQUES

An outline of the techniques is given below together with a note about two other approaches used by the Cheshire group of teachers participating in the Schools Council 'Effective Use of Reading' Project.

- Underlining. This is designed to focus attention on one aspect of the content or the language of a text. Generally speaking one would expect the focus of attention in Science texts to be content, in English texts, language, and in Humanities either may be appropriate.
- Word Deletion. Selected words are removed from the text after careful prior consideration. The technique should not be confused with cloze procedure which is a method of regular deletion for readability assessment; nor should it be confused with comprehension testing. It is a device to encourage pupils to think about meaning.
- Labelling. 'Labels' are headings or annotation that pupils may use to identify, classify or group features or information in the content of a text. They may also be required to invent their own labels to summarise, reorganise or represent an original text.
- Scrambled Texts. By scrambling, the original ordering of a sequence, process or plot is re-

shuffled. Criteria of logic may guide the scrambling of non-fiction texts whereas fiction or poetry texts may be scrambled according to literary or linguistic criteria.

Two further techniques are included in the present book:

- Group Prediction. Pupils are presented with a text in successive stages so that they have to 'guess' what happens next in a narrative or exposition.
- Re-presentation. This involves pupils in re-presenting a text in something other than its original shape or form. It may well be an appropriate later stage to labelling and makes demands on the pupil as an interpreter of language. It is worth noting here that some members of the group regarded the exercise of labelling as one which, apparently simple at first, involved pupils in potentially difficult and far reaching conceptual learning e.g. what is the difference between factual information and expressions of opinion? Are there, for example, different kinds of facts?

Excerpt from 'Reading for Learning in the Secondary School', published by Cheshire Language Centre.

Appendix Three

# SELECT BIBLIOGRAPHY

This bibliography has been arranged in chronological order to give an overview of the development of ideas in the first half of the 1980s.

1980

Papert, S. Mindstorms: Children, Computers and Powerful Ideas (Harvester Press). Still an essential introduction to the chief educational and philosophical questions, and much more besides.

1981

Chandler, D. Are We Still Living in Lagado? (MEP). The text of a lecture on relationships between microelectronics and the humanities.

Sharples, M. 'A Computer-based Teaching Scheme for Creative Writing', in R. Lewis and D. Tagg (eds.) Computers in Education (North Holland Publishing Co).

1982

Chandler, D. 'The Potential of the Microcomputer in the English Classroom' in A. Adams (ed.) New Directions in English Teaching (Falmer Press).

1983

Chandler, D. (ed.). Exploring English with Microcomputers, published by the Council for Educational Technology in association with the National Association for the Teaching of English. A collection of papers discussing classroom practice and observation of children using computers.

Adams, A. and Jones, E. Teaching Humanities in the Microelectronic Age (Open University Press).

1984

Chandler, D. Young Learners and the Microcomputer (Oxford University Press). A stimulating introduction not only to the use of computers in the primary school but to a newly emerging style and philosophy of teaching and learning.

Smith, F. The Promise and the Threat of Microcomputers in Language Education (published by the Centre for the Teaching of Reading, University of Reading, 29, Eastern Avenue, Reading). The last paragraph almost says it all: 'If teachers and children are able to make use of the creative and interactive potential, then I believe we are on the threshold of a world of learning scarcely imaginable. The alternative is the employment of computers in ways that will destroy literacy. And teachers alone must decide and assert the way computers will be used in education.' A love-hate relationship shared by many teachers!

1985

Sharples, M. Cognition, Computers and Creative Writing (Ellis Horwood Press). The first comprehensive look at microcomputers and writing in terms of the thinking process behind the writing.

Robinson, B. Microcomputers and the Language Arts (Open University Press).

Chandler, D. and Marcus, S. Computers and Literacy (Open University Press).

See also The English Magazine, No.15 (published by The English Centre, Sutherland Street, London W1). It contains articles on word processing software.

1986

Creative Uses of Word Processors, An interim report of an MEP curriculum development (published by the Cheshire Language Centre, North Cheshire College, Warrington). Compares different approaches to classroom use.

English Teaching and the New Technology (published by NATE). This document summarises the conclusion reached by the Cambridge Seminar, October 1985.

Micro-Explorations 2: Evaluating and Using Language and Reading Software, edited by Wray, and Potter, F. for the United Kingdom Reading Association. A companion volume to the UKRA papers mentioned in Chapter One.

Appendix Four

## A LIST OF PROGRAMS AND PUBLISHERS

AMAZING, G. Chadwick, North Cheshire College, Warrington, Cheshire.
CASTLE OF RIDDLES, Acornsoft.
DEVELOPING TRAY, MEP.
DIET, MEP.
EDFAX, MEP.
ELECTRONIC NEWS, Nottingham Educational Supplies.
FACTFILE, Cambridge Micro Software and MEP.
FLEET STREET EDITOR, Mirrorsoft.
FRONT PAGE, MAPE.
GRANNY'S GARDEN, 4mation.
HALVING, MEP.
THE HOBBIT, Melbourne.
MAKE ADVENTURE, MEP.
MICROSTORY, ESM.
MICROWORD, John Stout, Cusp Computers, 15, Hoghton Street, Southport, Merseyside.
MIKEFAX, Colin Rowling, 2 Tamar Close, Haydock, Merseyside.
PODD, ESM.
POEM-WRITER, Malcolm Glover, Thelwall Junior School, Warrington, Cheshire.
SPACEX, 4mation.
SUPASTORE, ESM.
SWITCHIT, MEP.
WELLIES, Cheshire Language Centre, North Cheshire College, Warrington, Cheshire.
WORDPLAY, MEP.
WORDWEB, ESM.
WORDWISE PLUS, Computer Concepts.
WRITING MASTER, utility programs for WORDWISE PLUS in classroom use, D.M. Vaughan Edwards, Birchwood High School, Birchwood, Warrington, WA3 7PT.
WULFSTAN'S WORDHOARD, ESM.

## INDEX